WORSHIP ♥ MATTERS

A Moving Word

Media Art in Worship

Eileen D. Crowley

Augsburg Fortress

A MOVING WORD
Media Art in Worship

Unless otherwise indicated, Scripture quotations are from the New Revised Standard Version Bible © 1989 Division of Christian Education of the National Council of the Churches of Christ in the United States of America. Used by permission.

Editors: Suzanne Burke, Jessica Hillstrom
Cover and interior design: Laurie Ingram, Diana Running
Cover photos: beach at sunset, photo © PhotoDisc, Inc.; wheat, photo © Digital Vision, Ltd.

ISBN 0-8066-5286-1 / 978-0-8066-5286-3

Manufactured in the U.S.A.

10   09   08   07   06   1   2   3   4   5   6   7   8   9   10

Contents

Preface

The arts serve the word." That heading from principle 11 of the Evangelical Lutheran Church in America's statement on the practice of word and sacrament, *The Use of the Means of Grace*, sums up not only the role of music, two-dimensional visual arts, sculpture, textile art, drama, dance, and architecture for worship. It also sums up the role of a form of art typically not counted among the sacred arts—media art.

What is media art? It is moving art. It is not media technology being used just to create an image or to capture action on film or video. It involves people employing media technologies and artistic skills in the service of revelation.

Media art is a projected photograph that makes us see for the first time something that has previously escaped our vision. It is a combination of images and sounds that whizzes by our consciousness on a video monitor but that leaves a permanent impression in our memory. It is a song juxtaposed with film footage that does not match the lyrics, the unexpected combination of which causes us to wrestle with possible meaning and, suddenly, triggers an insight.

We encounter media art as light and sound. Where? It may be displayed on a video or computer screen or be projected onto cinema-size projection screens. It often involves the combination of multiple forms of media: still and moving images, animation, graphics, music, and words spoken and provided as text to be read. Michael Rush calls this combination "new media" (*New Media in Art*, 2005). When we experience new media in a museum or exhibition, we often are invited to enjoy media art that dances across an arrangement of display or projection surfaces. On such occasions, we typically are invited to participate in some way with what in the art world is called a video or media installation. We are part of the art.

When we listen to recorded music, watch TV, attend a movie, surf the Internet, or visit a family entertainment theme park, we encounter media art of many kinds. Whether produced by amateurs or professionals, though, media art is more than the sum of the equipment used to create it. Media art is art born of technical skills, imagination, attention to aesthetics, and an intention to communicate more than words alone can say.

We experience media art in our homes, schools, workplaces, convention halls, shopping malls, and public spaces. We just may never have called it "media art."

Media art in the twenty-first century "paints" with pulsating light and energy. On a video monitor, media art may look still, such as a still photograph or graphic. In actuality, video is made up of pulses of red, green, and blue light that race by our eyes so fast we cannot see the individual pulses. We only see the pattern they create: an image. This medium is illusory, ephemeral, gone before we know it. Most times, we cannot go back and "re-read" what we missed. It is an art in motion.

Video is one form of media art, typically produced using video cameras and computer graphics and editing software. The video—whether broadcast or stored on videotape or DVD—plays across a video monitor or media screen. Consider for a moment the origin of that word *video*. It comes from the Latin word for "I see." In theological terms, this term seems especially appropriate for this media art. Video brings before our eyes and into our ears sights and sounds from worlds to which we may never travel bodily. It places us in the eye of a hurricane and in the midst of the grieving people devastated by its path. It puts us into the firefight of battles on the other side of the globe. It makes us witnesses to the miracle of birth. It captures for our grandchildren and great-grandchildren moments in the lives of long-gone grandparents whom they otherwise would never have had a chance to meet.

For more than a century, individual worship leaders have introduced media art into their congregation's worship. Projected slides and silent movies were welcomed into some Protestant services in the early decades of the twentieth century. Since the late 1970s, more and more church leaders in the United States and elsewhere have outfitted their worship spaces with projection technology and surfaces for the display of lyrics, prayers, scripture passages, sermon illustrations, announcements, videotaped testimonies, film clips, short documentaries, and mission reports. In these churches media projection aids in worshipers' participation, provides information, and offers inspiration. However, "the use of electronic media and technology in a worship space presents both opportunities and challenges for the church's worship" (principle S-15, *Principles for Worship*, Renewing Worship, vol. 2, 2002). This essay addresses that reality, because worship matters, and how we use media technology and art in worship matters, too.

Our focus shall *not* be on media technology. Many consultants are eager to help you sort through the wide range of media technologies available for your church. A major international electronics company recently named a national sales representative exclusively for the "houses of worship" market. Media technology for worship is a multi-faceted business with vendors across the country ready to educate you and to offer media hardware and software solutions for your worship space.

Rather, we shall concentrate on a single aspect of this phenomenon: how we can employ the media of many arts to produce media *art* that can serve God and your congregation as a *liturgical art*. We shall consider media art in worship in relationship to the Evangelical Lutheran Church in America's *Principles for Worship*, especially those principles and applications related to worship space (noted in parentheses after each quotation). Highlighting a particular aspect of media in worship that has received little attention—media art for meditation—we shall imagine how media art might serve liturgy throughout the liturgical year.

Why these foci? "The visual arts and forms of media embody and support the proclamation of the word of God" (principle S-16). Media art combines light, sound, and motion in ways that can move us emotionally and stir our imaginations. In worship, media art that truly is liturgical art also has the potential to provide "a portal to the mystery of God," because it can bring beauty into our worship (principle S-20). Media art in worship can become "a moving word" as powerful as any well-proclaimed passage of scripture or well-prayed liturgical text. It can occasion an encounter with the one who is Beauty. Like all liturgical arts, media art can truly be a means of grace.

1

Prepare the Way

Darkness. Candles flickering. People waiting in silence. The wind blowing, even howling. Simple instrumental music. Chant crossing the aisle in waves from one group to another. Icons illuminated.

To those who have celebrated the ecumenical Taizé style of evening prayer—with its elements of darkness, scores of candles, long silences, chant, intercessory prayer, and simple melodies matched to a few lines of lyrics in Latin and other languages, and little (if any) physical movement—the mood of Advent is not unknown. Both Taizé services and the season of Advent involve our experiencing a pregnant time, filled with anticipation, waiting, attending.

> Prepare the way of the Lord.
> Prepare the way of the Lord,
> and all people will see the salvation of our God.
> (Taizé Community, 1984)

During a visit to Toronto, I happened one evening to walk by an Anglican church on the way to my hotel room. Seeing a sign announcing Taizé prayer, I decided to go in and join this Canadian community. I was early. I sat toward the back, unsure how long I would stay. I looked through the worship aid I had found waiting on a small table as I had entered. Some of the chants I knew, others not. Other braver souls, one by one, walked toward the front. Perhaps 30 people drifted in and took their places at varying distances from the altar. At some point music began, and those gathered started the hauntingly simple refrains of a chant from the Taizé repertoire. I had attended Taizé services before, and have since. But as I reflect now on the possibilities for a moving word that can be liturgical media art, the openness, simplicity, and meditative quality of this ecumenical form of prayer comes to mind.

People, especially young people, have gravitated to this multilingual meditative form of worship for decades now. In North America, such services do not draw quite the same crowd as does the worship at the abbey at Taizé. Thousands of pilgrims from around the world flock to pray with this ecumenical community in France. In parishes Lutheran, Episcopal, and Roman Catholic, worshipers sometimes do gather, especially in the night, for Advent and Lenten services that follow some variation of the Taizé service model and sing their chants. Why do people come? To pray in a form that encourages meditation and openness to the Spirit. Some people find as they repeat the chants over and over again that they enter a contemplative space within themselves that is not opened in quite the same way in their experience of Sunday worship. The music can induce a trance-like atmosphere as people dwell deeper and deeper in the sung prayer. Some find peace.

> Come and fill our hearts with your peace.
> You alone, O Lord, are holy.
> Come and fill our hearts with your peace.
> Alleluia!
> (Taizé Community, 1982, 1991)

In North American culture that encourages filled-in daily schedules and overcommitted lives, it is fair to say that time for meditation does not typically get assigned one of the blocks on one's computer calendar, unless a person is a practitioner of Buddhism, yoga, or a secularized form of transcendental meditation. To people living frantically filled days, a night in the candlelit darkness and undulating chants of Taizé may at first be disconcerting, even discomforting. Way too much stillness. Way too much silence. To those people who need to be in perpetual motion, meditation can be an utterly foreign experience. And yet, even the frantic sometimes walk through church doors into these services and let their tensions dissolve as they gradually allow themselves to engage a focus that is Other-centered. They are moved by the words carried aloft on melodies that seem to have no real ending.

> Wait for the Lord whose day is near.
> Wait for the Lord: be strong, take heart!
> (Taizé Community, 1984)

Meditation is an art, as well as a practiced discipline. It requires structure, yet leads to structurelessness. It involves attending to the moment, yet also entering into time-out-of-time. During a service, people can come to attune themselves not only to the Taizé melodies, but also to an awareness of their dwelling as a people united in sung prayer, gathered in the midst of God-with-us, Emmanuel.

Media meditations

> Deep calls to deep at the thunder of your cataracts;
> all your waves and your billows have gone over me. (Ps. 42:7)

The ability to dwell with, to attend, to attune oneself, to respond to the call of the Deep can be an unexpected discovery for people who are ever on the move. For them, and for others too, awaits another occasion for meditation: media meditations within worship. When crafted as simply, gracefully, artfully, and hauntingly as a Taizé chant, media art can likewise invite and potentially draw people into an encounter with the Holy One. Media meditations can be integral to many kinds of prayer services, including Taizé services.

Meditative services at Prince of Peace Lutheran Church in Burnsville, Minnesota, have tried to create a "space for God" through juxtaposed projections of religious art and icons with Taizé and other kinds of chants, including chants locally composed. A single image may remain throughout a chant, or several may slowly dissolve one to another. This large contemporary worship space contains many strong visual symbols: the table, reading desk, baptismal font, cross, leaded stained glass, and many candles. "But the projection is able to take us beyond those and add to the media palette," explains Handt Hanson, director of worship arts. Sometimes a camera focuses in on what is already in the space, such as the leaded glass window portraying the Lord's Prayer, and projects this liturgical art during prayer "so all can engage with it as we pray with our eyes open." Meditative music for the ears and projected art for meditation of the eyes can combine to give worshipers multiple ways to enter into Absolute Mystery. This combination of two forms of "moving words"—aural and visual—is a simple example of media art for worship.

Yes, media art in worship can be as simple as a well-chosen, well-composed, well-placed projected photograph or other image that serves as the focus of a community's meditation, with or without music. Perhaps you have been part of creating meditative slide shows for youth or other gatherings. If the images you selected added another dimension to worship that otherwise would not have been possible with music or words alone, and if those images helped people to contemplate God's grace in some way, you have created liturgical media art.

Companies and church-related organizations sell CDs and DVDs filled with media images and video clips. Some media-for-worship providers allow you to purchase and to download individual files of media you wish to use in your community's worship. Conduct an Internet search for "media for worship," and you'll discover the variety of options available. If you want to use media in your worship, you don't need to be a talented photographer or have a media producer in your congregation. You just need to be a discerning online shopper, or to be skilled at finding copyright-free art on the Internet. Given the wealth of media art for worship available, integrating media art into your liturgy could seem to be a simple matter. You pick a theme, look online for sample clips on vendors' Web sites, select a photo or video file, and download it directly into your computer. You're all set, right? Wrong. The use of media art in worship *begins* with *worship,* not with an Internet hunt for media art treasures

Basic principles

Principles for Worship is wise in this regard: "Media serves liturgy." Look at application S-15A in the section devoted to worship space:

> The use of audiovisual elements in worship requires **careful consideration**. Such media are desirable when they **enhance** rather than replace essential **congregational action**. Their function of assisting the assembly's participation in worship through the visual arts may include providing the color and form of seasonal artwork. Because of the many ramifications of the use of this technology in worship, **careful integration** must be assured [emphasis added].

"Careful consideration" involves the weighing of multiple factors. It requires discernment. Let's take the case of an Advent service, whether it is an evening prayer or a Taizé or Iona-style service. First of all, whom do you hope will come to pray? The answer to the question "Who?" is always important, as any leader of prayer knows. Given that basic information, the answer to the next question of "What?" involves knowing the order of the service in which people will be invited to worship. How does the liturgy flow, for example, from music to spoken text to silence? If you were to analyze the whole trajectory of a service as you would a whole concerto, from an energy or an emotional standpoint, where does the liturgy rise and fall? Within that larger arc, what "congregational action" can be enhanced? At what points are worshipers externally active in speaking, singing, or moving? At what points are they internally active in listening, reflecting, or contemplating? Then there is the question of "Why?" What are the purposes of that liturgy's various elements: thanksgiving, praise, petition, confession, lament?

What are the images that rise up from the liturgical texts and from the scripture passages to be proclaimed? What hymns and songs might be incorporated appropriate to the service, this congregation, the liturgical season, and the context of this particular worship event? What metaphors do you find in their texts? What is the liturgical season and what images or metaphors are commonly associated with that season? What is the mood or atmosphere of this season? Answers to these questions lead to decisions about "the color and form of seasonal artwork," because in selecting or producing any media to include in worship you are potentially adding artwork into the worship space that your congregation will experience. (For an in-depth exploration of questions to ask in the process of creation, selection, incorporation, and evaluation of media in worship, see chapter 4 of *Liturgical Art in a Media Culture*.)

How might media "enhance rather than replace essential congregational action"? Projecting lyrics and prayer texts to encourage congregational participation is a common practice and is undoubtedly the most common use of media technology and software in worship. Where worshipers are asked to sing in a dimly lighted space, projection of lyrics and melody line aid the congregation . . . unless the electricity goes out, that is!

You will want to strive for liturgically based "careful integration," not merely incorporation. You would do best to avoid integration of media for the sake of entertainment, as a marketing strategy triggered by the example of a growing local church that uses media, or simply because worship leaders want to do something different. The starting point of any appropriate use of media in worship is not related to incorporation, because anyone can add visuals or video to a service. It is a matter of integrating media art in such a way that it serves liturgy and enhances people's experience of worship. It is a matter of media art helping people to pray and to encounter the divine

In sum, "careful consideration" and "careful integration" of media in worship must start with the liturgy and those who pray it. If you do not reflect on these basics, integration of media technology and media art may be inappropriate or poorly timed. It may be experienced as superfluous or jarring. It can end up being media *in* worship, but not media *of* worship.

Imagine . . .

Given these basic principles, now it is your turn to apply them. Consider how you might integrate into an Advent service the following video vignette offered by Highway Video, entitled, "Oh Come, Oh Come Emmanuel." View this video at www.highwayvideo.com by selecting "Seasonal Highway Video/Elements" and then "Christmas Singles." This haunting four-minute piece begins with an outside shot of a modest suburban ranch house, followed by interior shots of the house that ultimately take us to the bedroom of the owner. He awakens, gets up slowly, and begins to go through his morning routine as we hear a piano and a single voice singing plaintively the ancient chant, "Oh, come, oh, come, Emmanuel." Thanks to a series of tight shots, we put together the telling details provided and suspect who he is. This gentleman is a white-bearded, bespeckled man of an age and shape to fit the stereotype of what we have come to expect of Santa Claus. But this is no jolly old Saint Nick, and he has by no means a cheery start to his day. He brushes his teeth, cooks a single egg, and eats a simple breakfast with only a program on a small TV set in the corner of his kitchen to keep him company. It is evident he is all alone. The way the director has shot the footage and lighted the scenes, much in extreme close-up and in silhouette, well suits the lyrics, "disperse the gloomy clouds of night, and death's dark shadows put to flight." We watch as he takes down a box that turns out to contain a Santa Claus suit. He dons his costume. Lost in thought he looks through the curtains to the world outside. He polishes his boots, finishes his coffee, plops into a glass of water two tablets of an antacid that fizzes. He departs through his front door, now dressed in full Santa Claus attire, to the refrain of "Rejoice! Rejoice! Emmanuel shall come to you, O Israel." We see him get into his late-model car, then arrive at a shopping mall. Out he steps to take on the role of the eternal jolly one, but as he heads to the store entry he looks to be a person who will find it difficult to offer the expected "Ho ho ho."

The Highway Video Web site copy accompanying this clip asks: "Are you able to rejoice in the coming of Emmanuel? How can you share the true story of the birth of God without coming to terms with your own struggles, loneliness, and regret? Have you betrayed the mysterious joy of Christmas for the commercial mystique of Christmas?" The holiday season is surely a painful time for many people who are experiencing grief, separation from loved ones, illness, or depression. The pressure of advertisements that emphasize gift-giving may make those on tight budgets feel inadequate. Because they cannot afford the items on their children's "wish lists" parents may feel they have failed their loved ones. For a variety of reasons, during Advent (and Christmas) many in our congregations may be silently struggling to find a reason to rejoice.

Knowing the pain present in so many parishioners' hearts, how might this vignette be sensitively and appropriately incorporated into a service? How might this video lead into or out of prayer, song, or sermon? The vignette, the work of Highway Video founder

Travis Reed and his new production group called The Work of the People (www.theworkofthepeople.com), is an example of media art for worship. It only becomes *liturgical* media art when it serves the liturgy and draws the congregation more deeply into participating in the mystery we celebrate as God-with-us, Emmanuel. Depending on how, when, where, and why it is used in an Advent liturgy, this ancient text and medieval tune, already layered in our memories of Advents past, may take on another layer of associations. For some members of the congregation, an element of Advent worship so often taken for granted could become a "moving word" heard again for the first time.

For reflection and discussion

1. How are media technology and media art now being used in your congregation's worship or in that of neighboring congregations? What have you heard reported about media in worship from people who have experienced it? If you have had such experiences, how did you find it helped or hindered your ability to pray?

2. How might media art of any kind help your community prepare the way of the Lord?

3. What passage from the Advent lectionary readings might you wish to see interpreted as a media meditation?

4. Recall a time when a scene in a movie or TV program or on a news report moved you. Why did it? What was it about the story or the way it was produced that touched you? Have you ever been moved to such an extent that you took some action because of what you experienced via media?

5. How might the integration of the video vignette "Oh Come, Oh Come Emmanuel" affect your Advent worship and your understanding of this liturgical season?

2
Let There Be Light!

Arise, shine; for your light has come, and the glory of the LORD has risen upon you. For darkness shall cover the earth, and thick darkness the peoples; but the LORD will arise upon you, and his glory will appear over you.
—Isa. 60:1-2, from the first reading for Epiphany of Our Lord

They set out; and there, ahead of them, went the star that they had seen at its rising, until it stopped over the place where the child was. When they saw that the star had stopped, they were overwhelmed with joy.
—Matt. 2:9-10, from the gospel for Epiphany of Our Lord

In the beginning when God created the heavens and the earth, the earth was a formless void and darkness covered the face of the deep. . . . Then God said, "Let there be light"; and there was light. And God saw that it was good; and God separated the light from the darkness.
—Gen. 1:1-4, from the first reading for Baptism of Our Lord, year B

In those days Jesus came from Nazareth of Galilee and was baptized by John in the Jordan. And just as he was coming up out of the water, he saw the heavens torn apart and the Spirit descending like a dove on him.
—Mark 1:9-10, from the gospel for Baptism of Our Lord, year B

In the exhaustion after Christmas and New Year celebrations, two liturgical celebrations often get short shrift: Epiphany and Baptism of Our Lord. Too bad. Located in the midst of the shortest days and longest nights, these two winter feasts could both be subtitled, "Let there be light!" Light in darkness, stars in the sky, night and day, the heavens opening up, and the Light of the world shine forth from our scripture readings. These occasions in deep winter in the Northern Hemisphere are, very appropriately, a time when a congregation could use the art that is made of light, media art.

Communal Co-creation of liturgical media art

Preparation for these liturgies needs to be done well in advance, of course, whether media art is an element or not. After the holidays, pastors and members who usually work together on worship for Advent and Christmas often find themselves running out of energy. They simply may not be able to deal with preparing anything special for one more feast. Given that possibility, they might invite a different group—parish adults, teens, and children—to serve as a special worship team just for these liturgies. In late September or early October, perhaps, an invitation might be sent to particular individuals known to be imaginative or to have art backgrounds, and to the rest of the congregation: "We would like to celebrate Epiphany and the Baptism of Our Lord in a special way this year and would welcome your helping to make this happen. Come to a meeting this Wednesday to reflect on these feasts in relationship to your experience of art, poetry, movies, TV, photography, music, and today's popular media in general. Bring along a friend and your imagination, and we'll provide the cookies!"

This invitation could be the start of a parish process I call "Communal Co-creation." The idea behind this process is simple. Liturgy is not solely the responsibility of the pastor. It is the action of the whole community. Just as Lutherans know that singing is their responsibility as an assembly, so too through the process of Communal Co-creation some worshipers might come to appreciate more deeply that the entire liturgy is theirs. Why not call upon the people to prepare for their own worship? "Art and architecture proclaim the gospel, enrich the assembly's participation in the word and sacraments, and reinforce the themes of the occasion and season. Liturgical art animates the life and faith of the community" (principle S-5). Why not invite people to create liturgical media art that animates the life and faith of their community? In our hypothetical case, pastors could invite parishioners to develop services in which media art is integral to the proclamation of the word as liturgical art, not as an add-on. As I have seen in congregations around the country, collaboration of this sort can happen. In some communities it occurs even weekly.

Whom might you recruit? Who might respond? The Holy Spirit might inspire people you would never expect to volunteer, people who have never been on any church committee. Included in this team could be people especially skilled in art: "Artists, amateur and professional, are encouraged to collaborate with worship leaders and seasonal planning teams so that their work is focused on the assembly and its worship" (application S-5F). Today, people of nearly all ages have experience with media art, and many have developed skills in photography, videography, and photo- and video-editing. Musicians, poets, computer techies, movie fans, and TV buffs could join school teachers and children, graphic artists, new and long-time members, good organizers, and generous folks of every kind. Guided by the pastor or another with training in worship planning and spiritual reflection, members of this special worship team could bring their diverse gifts and collective imaginations to bear on these two liturgies. In the course of plumbing the depths of these liturgies, people who participate in Communal Co-creation would find themselves engaged in a spiritual practice that ultimately can enrich their own worship life, as well as that of other members of the congregation. How might members of a special Communal Co-creation team go about their task?

Imagine what could happen . . .

It's Wednesday night, and a diverse group of people sits around a table ready to start thinking about the Epiphany and Baptism of Our Lord liturgies. You are facilitating this brainstorming session. As with any worship planning session, participants involved in this special project begin by reading and reflecting upon the scripture and liturgical prayers assigned for these feasts in relationship to their daily lives. They review the texts of the hymns selected for those celebrations and talk about how those songs have affected them in the past. Someone mentions a movie that the songs have brought to mind. That association leads you to offer a bit of education on media art.

"Many people associate media in worship with what they have seen in preaching or praise and worship services: projected lyrics, prayers, scripture passages, or theme-based graphics." They agree that this assessment has been their experience and their expectation of what this gathering is about. You respond that, although those approaches are common in the use of media in worship, other possibilities exist. You tell them about the option of creating media meditations that can add something entirely different to worship, a time for reflection. They are intrigued, but a bit confused. How would someone create a media meditation? And what would it be?

To illustrate the possibilities, you invite team members to look at the popular Epiphany hymn, "O Morning Star, how fair and bright!" You ask them where in their lives they have experienced manifestations of "God's own truth and light, aglow with grace and mercy." Individuals recall a news report, a popular song, or a movie scene that featured people who had gone out of their way to be light for others in the darkness of disaster, disease, despair, or depression. You have brought along newspapers. You ask everyone to take a section and scan the pages for headlines and photos that might provide visual material for a black-and-white media meditation for this song. After some time for that exercise, the participants call out their candidates.

A visual artist is present. You ask her how she might go about interpreting this song. She talks about how her creative process might lead her to do a series of sketches. Right then and there, she goes to a flip chart and demonstrates the kinds of images already jumping out at her from the song and the Epiphany readings. You ask a photographer how he might go about the same creative task, and he shares his process. The group discusses what might happen if the artist's sketches or the photographer's work were videotaped and then shown on Epiphany as the prelude or call to worship, accompanied by an instrumental version of this hymn.

Next, you ask the group to try to re-imagine the magi. Who might they be today? Some of the teens get into this topic. Other participants are surprised by the many people through whom the teens say they have been guided "to thy perfect light." A few of the teens end up offering to tackle producing their own hip-hop music video of "We three kings of Orient are."

A high school English teacher recalls the evocative T. S. Eliot poem, "The Journey of the Magi," in which one of the magi recalls the hardships and surprise of that journey. She has brought a copy of it along and reads it to the group. The participants agree that creating media art based on that poem might be daunting, but a challenge worth considering. A photographer suggests the possibility of shooting a series of images for a multimedia meditation on the wise ones of all ages and races who bear gifts in unexpected ways. As a reflection on this feast, an art lover has brought along a small collection of post cards and art reproductions that depict Epiphany in different styles and from different cultures. He passes them around to those at the table. Here is a way in which "embracing artistic and architectural styles from a variety of cultures enriches worship and encourages a broader experience of the church catholic" (application S-3C).

You affirm all of these wonderful ideas and confirm that, ultimately, only a few will likely end up in your parish worship. But that is okay, the group agrees. Better to have more ideas and more options so that the best might surface. Who knows what might come of all these first fruits of their discussion! Already they are beginning to see what might be possible . . . and the conversation becomes more and more animated.

You redirect their focus to the Baptism of Our Lord. You go through the same process of considering the relationship of the lectionary texts and prayers to what is happening in individuals' lives, the parish, and the rest of the world. A church musician present points out that for both feasts "Shine, Jesus, shine" might provide inspiration for a media meditation. Yes, we have light images in the scripture readings for both feasts.

The Baptism of Our Lord adds the element of water. A person from the environment committee mentions that they are hoping to have a large clear glass bowl on a pedestal at the entry to the worship space. Their baptismal font is so small, so shallow, and so out of the way that they feel it does not serve the kind of baptisms they hope will become common: immersion of infants, at least. And, although it is too soon to know whether anyone will be baptized on that feast, that Sunday is one of the Sundays when a baptismal festival might occur.

> The sacred touches people in the ordinary. God is present throughout creation. Effective use of natural light, flowing water, plants, and other natural materials contributes to our experience of the sacred. (application S-4E)

The conversation continues and participants start to reflect on water.

Options

A liturgist's fantasy? Yes. A possibility? Yes! Worth considering? Only you can answer that. But, I ask, what pastor would not love to have so many people around a table eager and willing to engage in this kind of lively conversation! Here are some other options a group like this might consider.

In worship spaces where flowing water from a baptismal font or pool does not exist, members could create a well-composed, well-edited video of local streams and rivers with the ambient sounds of gurgling and rushing waters as its only score. Temporary screens, stretched scrim or other translucent fabric, or reflective material such as Tyvek® might be positioned near the entry or by the baptismal font. A media screen that unrolls from the floor level might work, too. As the footage is projected onto that surface, a choir might be singing the syncopated "Waterlife" or the jazz composition, "I'm going on a journey." Whenever Prince of Peace Lutheran Church in Burnsville, Minnesota, uses "Waterlife," it is accompanied with purchased footage of moving water that comes as a part of a software package for media ministry, MediaShout (www.mediashout.com).

The well-known Genesis passage for the Baptism of Our Lord, year B, might entice someone interested in astronomy to assemble a series of photographs of galaxies and other images of the heavens to accompany the proclamation of this creation story, or to serve as environmental art during an organ prelude evocative of this light-and life-giving divine act.

Let the children come to me

The Baptism of Our Lord is among those days particularly appropriate for baptism. The premier occasion is the Vigil of Easter; other times include the Day of Pentecost and All Saints Sunday. A parish might choose to celebrate baptismal festivals on these or other days when water is the primary image in the day's scripture. If so, consider what this sacramental occasion might mean for the youngest members of your community.

When an infant baptism is celebrated during Sunday eucharist, some congregations make sure that children in Sunday school or in a separate age-appropriate celebration of the word come back to the main assembly in time to witness the baptism. Pastors sometimes invite children to gather close to the font so they can easily see this important event. In doing so, children can begin to understand that they are responsible for this baby, too. "An understanding of the physical and experiential needs of children contributes to the design of liturgy and liturgical spaces that are inviting to all" (application S-17C).

One way of giving children an opportunity to prepare for such times is to read to them the gospel story of Jesus' baptism and to invite them to draw pictures of flowing water and of Jesus in the Jordan, or to illustrate the musical acclamation, "You have put on Christ." Middle school children or teens could then produce a multimedia meditation by scanning the younger children's artwork, arranging the images in some kind of story line, and perhaps even adding a recording of the children singing the acclamation. For other baptisms, this media art could be used as the community welcomes the infant to the celebration of holy baptism, as the family approaches the font, or as a joyful burst of acclamation after the baptism as the whole community welcomes its new member. It is not a case of art for art's sake, or even of children's art for children's sake. It is an opportunity for the communal creation of media art that is appropriate and integral to worship. As *Principles for Worship* explains: "Art that draws attention to itself as an independent element tends to distract from the community's worship. Artwork created by children and communal artistic efforts are used effectively when integrated into a plan that reinforces the liturgy and the worship space" (application S-16D).

Children's art is important in the life of the church, and including it in worship teaches children that they, too, have gifts to offer to God and to God's church. If well-produced, a short baptismal media meditation featuring children's art might be shown to parents who are meeting to prepare for their child's baptism, or it could appear on the church's Web site. Many of the media meditations produced for specific liturgies—if they are well-focused around a single metaphor or image—can be used outside of worship in religious education and newcomers' classes, thereby connecting liturgy and life.

For reflection and discussion

1. If Communal Co-creation of media for worship were introduced in your congregation, how might an invitation go out that would attract the greatest diversity of people? How could you reach those members who seldom come to Sunday worship, who for whatever reasons stay on the margins of the life of your community?

2. In addition to the pastor, who within your community could facilitate the scriptural, liturgical, and theological reflection envisioned in this chapter?

3. How might Communal Co-creation be the occasion for outreach to people new to your parish or to people who live with physical or developmental disabilities? Since they, too, live in our media culture, they undoubtedly would have ideas to share.

4. How might immigrants be welcomed into Communal Co-creation and invited to share their stories about being guided "by thy perfect light"? How might their journey stories be turned into media testimonies?

5. Who within your community possesses skills in the arts—photography, graphic design, film or video production? What would it take to attract them to participation in Communal Co-creation?

6. If you were part of a worship team reflecting on Epiphany or Baptism of Our Lord, what hymn or song would you propose as the starting point for inspiration for the selection or creation of media meditations for your services?

3
Return to the Lord

It is another Wednesday night, and parishioners are gathering. But, this time, it is February, and they are gathering not around a conference table but around the altar. Sixty or so parishioners have made a special effort to come to church. It is Ash Wednesday. Some of them come because receiving ashes is a childhood custom they have continued. Some are former Roman Catholics. Others who grew up Lutheran have in recent years discovered that the parish's Ash Wednesday service is a good way to begin Lent.

People sit in silence. A musician from a nearby temple walks deliberately to the front of the assembly. He turns to the assembly, puts a *shofar* to his lips, and blows a series of long, wailing, and short blasts that Christians ordinarily do not hear, because these are the sounds of the Jewish High Holy Days. For Jews attending services, *shofar* blasts accompany an intense time of their standing before God and being honest about their lives and their failings. The musician departs. A voice from the choir loft announces:

> *Blow the trumpet in Zion; sound the alarm on my holy mountain! Let all the inhabitants of the land tremble, for the day of the*

Lord is coming, it is near—a day of darkness and gloom, a day of clouds and thick darkness! (Joel 2:1-2a)

On a screen to one side of the altar, video footage appears showing people walking along a crowded city street. Then, on a screen on the opposite side of the altar runs footage of cars streaming along highways. We hear the sounds of footsteps and traffic. The tempo of the footage on both sides gradually increases until the people and the cars are racing. All the while, the voice continues to proclaim the passage from Joel. Suddenly, to the crescendoing sound of honking horns and screeching tires, the footage on both sides freezes on a blur of motion that dissolves into a heap of ashes. Silence. The voice firmly declares:

Yet even now, says the Lord, return to me with all your heart, with fasting, with weeping, and with mourning; rend your hearts and not your clothing. Return to the Lord, your God, for he is gracious and merciful, slow to anger, and abounding in steadfast love, and relents from punishing. (Joel 2:12-13)

Silence. The pastor steps forward. The people stand.

In the name of the Father, and of the Son, and of the Holy Spirit.

The pastor and people make the sign of the cross. The congregation adds its "Amen." The pastor continues:

Let us confess our sin in the presence of God and of one another.

Silence. Extensive silence. A time for reflection and self-examination. Then the pastor offers the prayer of the day:

Gracious God, out of your love and mercy you breathed into dust the breath of life, creating us to serve you and our neighbors. Call forth our prayers and acts of kindness, and strengthen us to face our mortality, with confidence in the mercy of your Son.

After the prayer, the pastor speaks of the early church, of how, in fifth-century Rome, Christians formally entering the ancient Order of Penitents would come before the bishop at the start of what became known as Lent; of how they would dress from then until Holy Thursday in sack cloth, with ashes sprinkled on their head or garment, as a sign of their sorrow for sin; of how, by the eleventh century, all Christians were expected to become penitents for Lent and to receive the mark of ashes upon their forehead as a sign of their desire to purify themselves in preparation for Easter. The pastor invites the congregation to do likewise and asks those in the back to be the first to come forward.

As people process to receive ashes on their foreheads in the shape of a cross, a cellist plays a well-known Jewish melody, "Kol Nidre," an ancient, mournful melody named after the opening prayer of Yom Kippur, the Day of Atonement. On the two media screens, the ashes dissolve into black-and-white images of people of all ages and races evidently in need, without sufficient food, clothing, or shelter; images of destitute, blighted neighborhoods that congregants recognize as being not that far away from their own homes; and other local images of extreme wealth juxtaposed against local images of extreme poverty. After everyone has come forward, the media screen footage ends on a single dark gray background with white text: "For where your treasure is, there your heart will be also" (Matt. 6:21).

Options

This imagined opening to an Ash Wednesday service depends upon pastor, musicians, and media ministers working together to set the tone for an entire liturgical season, Lent. It requires all liturgical leaders to collaborate closely in working through the connections among words, sounds, silences, and actions. It is most effective when every liturgical element is well-rehearsed and well-timed, and when the silences are deep.

Sometimes pastors make the mistake of thinking that any weekday service must be quick, because people are busy. But, just the opposite may be true. People come to these optional weekday services because they want and need them. They are seeking sustenance. They are not coming for spiritual fast food, but for spiritual nourishment that will fuel their efforts to return to God. Like all liturgies, the Ash Wednesday liturgy deserves great care, including care in how media art might be incorporated.

In addition to how media were used in our opening scenario, in what other ways might media art serve the Ash Wednesday liturgy? In brainstorming possible media ideas, planners might ask themselves, "What might rending hearts *sound* like?" They might turn to choral or well-known instrumental settings of Psalm 51, evocative music that might give some aural hints to lead them to an answer. "What would rending hearts *look* like?" Lenten hymn texts might provide images and metaphors that would fire up an artist's imagination. For the time in the liturgy when people process to be marked with ashes, worship planners might consider having a soloist chant a penitential litany with the people responding with the refrain, "Hold us in your mercy" (see, for example, Rory Cooney and Gary Daigle's "Hold Us in Your Mercy: Penitential Litany," published by GIA). Litanies work well when people are moving because they require no music in hand. Litanies also free eyes to see whatever media art might be offered, as in our opening example. If people are standing in line for a while or are waiting in their seats for their turn to come forward, they can be meditating on media art whose aural and visual content is suggestive of "rending hearts."

How media art functions

Media functions in so many ways in our lives and is such an integral part of our daily environments that we sometimes barely take note of it, and rarely analyze its many roles. In worship, media fills many of the roles that cluster around these five general functions:

- To encourage participation
- To convey information
- To reinforce and enrich oral communications
- To open up an interactive space—within or outside us—for discovery
- To provide beauty

The first three functions are primarily communications functions. Media art designed to get a message through to a congregation would qualify under these categories. It might offer what words they are to sing, what actions they are invited to take, what something being spoken about looks like or is analogous of. Media art that serves these first three functions may be executed with attention to aesthetic values, but it may or may not function in the final two ways. The last two functions move us into a new dimension of communications; they refer to media that function in ways beyond the instrumental. They refer to media that function as *art*. People experience this kind of media art as in some way inspirational or revelatory. It is media art that can be for worshipers a moving word.

Through the years I have analyzed how media art functions in many different forms of worship. The articulation of these five functions has proved helpful in conversations with pastors, congregation members, and graduate students in seminaries and schools of theology. Appreciating how media function allows people to begin to make distinctions, and being able to make distinctions is part of critical thinking. By "critical" I do not mean criticizing. I mean being able to analyze a situation against some relevant criteria.

Practical issues

Principles for Worship proposes criteria as the basis for reflection on media technologies and media art in worship. Some are simply practical, such as this:

> Technological equipment (sound boards, light systems, microphones, speakers, cameras, projectors, video screens) is most effective when it does not impair liturgical movement, obscure primary symbols (meal, preaching, baptism), or adversely affect the design of the space and its worship. (application S-15A)

Obviously we would not want our movement impaired as we make our way forward to receive ashes or communion. When it comes to our worship spaces, though, sometimes we do lose sight of such basic practicalities, because our minds are focused elsewhere. In adding media equipment to our sanctuary, we might become so enthralled with our new media technology that we fail to see how its placement does indeed get in the way. It can simply be in a bad spot, for example, in a place that blocks people's view or that makes it awkward for worshipers in motorized wheelchairs to move forward for communion.

In adding media equipment to a worship space, we might be tempted to install a remote-controlled screen that rolls down beautifully above the center aisle so all can see, but that covers up the historically significant cross that had been the focal point of the space. What does that say about a congregation's priorities? One congregation covered over a back wall of stained glass windows with its media screen. To compensate, whenever they were not showing text or graphics on the screen, they projected a photograph of the stained glass window that the congregation could no longer see. Such a sad solution. In worship spaces not originally designed as auditoriums, the question of where to place a screen for the projection of media can be difficult. If the only criterion for where to locate a screen is "Where do we put this so people can see?" other aesthetic criteria might be ignored. How does this screen or these screens work with or against the architecture of the church? In a Tudor-style church in California, two media screens literally blend into the woodwork.

During a renovation, the screens were boxed in by wood beams that were integral to the architectural design. The color of the surrounding walls is the same as that of the screens, so that when the screens are not actively in use they seem to disappear.

> Beyond its functional nature, a hospitable space is inviting because of the harmony of its materials, the scale of its proportions, and the integral nature of its parts. Excellent lighting and acoustics, space for liturgical interaction, absence of barriers, and well-crafted furnishing all contribute to hospitality. A hospitable room is not only a good place to worship, it is a good place to be. (application S-17A)

Even though technological media solutions may make worship less hospitable, some media technologies can make worship more hospitable by making liturgy more accessible to people, by making it "a good place to be" for *everyone*. "A hospitable worship space generously accommodates the assembly, its liturgy, and a broad range of activities appropriate to the life of the congregation and its surrounding community" (principle S-17). In creating hospitable spaces for all worshipers, media technology may serve liturgy in a way not yet mentioned. As *Principles for Worship* notes: "Media and technology can also assist in overcoming physical limitations, aid sight for the visually impaired, and augment sound for the hearing impaired, facilitating everyone's full participation" (application S-15B).

How big?

Surfaces on which to display or project media art come in many sizes. They need to be appropriate to the functions media art plays in a community's worship. Where a congregation is only using media to display text or an occasional graphic with text on it, the screens may not need to be too big—as long as the size of the text makes it easily readable by the persons sitting furthest away. In contrast, in circumstances where a congregation is using media art as environmental art, the projection or display surfaces may need to be more in number and much larger in size to allow people to feel surrounded or wrapped in those images and sounds. This latter situation is akin to that of gallery, museum, exhibition, shrine, or World's Fair kinds of spaces whose walls actually *are*, top-to-bottom and wall-to-wall, made entirely of media screens. Like a Gothic worship space such as the royal upper chapel of Sainte-Chapelle in Paris, whose walls are primarily composed of stained glass through which sunlight floods the space, media art can similarly surround worshipers and create an illuminating environment into which we enter to pray.

When deciding how big screens or monitors need to be, their location within the worship space is a factor. Their size and placement require careful consideration lest media art seem out of proportion to the physical space it occupies. Projected media may loom so large that they—rather than the liturgical action—become the center of attention. The scale of projection surfaces in relationship to the worshipers and to the architectural space itself needs careful consideration to prevent video screens—or preachers projected on them—from becoming today's new idols or media stars. At times, though, media projection or display surfaces may appropriately take center stage because of how the media function within a liturgy, as when it serves as media for meditation or as environmental art.

In working with our worship spaces, we need to keep in mind that these spaces can and do communicate. When we add the element of media screens or displays into these spaces, they, too, communicate. Ideally, "worship space witnesses to the gospel in ways that challenge destructive patterns within society and affirm justice, peace, and the integrity of God's creation" (principle S-6). We would not want the use of media in our worship spaces to reflect the destructive pattern we know as consumerism. The desire for better, more complex media equipment that exceeds the needs or resources of a community can lead to irresponsible stewardship or, at the very least, to poor decision making. I agree with Calvin College communications professor Quentin J. Schultze who calls for moderation in a church's "technological stewardship":

> The safest way to address technology-related costs is to practice reasonable moderation within the context of excellence—not perfection. Many consultants will advise that a church should spend as much as it can afford on presentational technologies to avoid disappointing performance and the need to replace equipment in the near future. In most worship spaces, however, higher-end equipment is unnecessary. (*High-Tech Worship? Using Presentational Technologies Wisely*, 2004, p. 79)

Location, location, location

While we are considering practical issues, let us address another one: where might media art be located in the worship space? Our opening Ash Wednesday scenario assumed the presence of media screens. Many other possibilities exist. In order to think through what would be most appropriate in their worship space and how they want media art to function in their services, worship planners might do well to reflect a bit on how they encounter media art in other kinds of public spaces. Let me give you an example.

A few years ago, I visited the Kerry Museum in Tralee, Ireland. I had recently completed my first book on aesthetics for liturgical media art, and so I was delighted by the very first room I entered. In a half-darkened space, we visitors from various countries walked in and selected a comfortable perch upon multilevel rocks (simulated) arranged to give the impression that we were sitting at a shoreline looking out onto the sea. Instead of the sea, though, we were treated to a ten-minute narration-free multimedia show projected on the opposite wall. A few titles in multiple languages, music, and sound effects guided us on an audiovisual tour across the local landscape.

Images of Kerry's mountains, lakes, pastures, forests, fauna, flora, and people offered us impressions of life in this particular part of southwestern Ireland and of those who had made this part of the world their home for millennia. This media art presentation, set within the larger imagination-stimulating environment of that room, welcomed us and set the tone for our self-guided tour. It introduced us visually and aurally to the rugged beauty and dancing sounds of this county. That multimedia presentation quickened our desire to see and to learn more and made it possible for us to be tuned in to what we were about to experience of Kerry's story.

Later on, toward the end of our meandering through exhibits, a video monitor in one of them offered footage from old black-and-white news reels. We watched moments from Irish uprisings and rebellions in the 1910s, struggles for nationhood, wars, poverty, and changes in political leadership. This series of film clips functioned similarly to the first multimedia welcome. This media art created an occasion for us to stop and to reflect. Having seen in exhibit after exhibit ample evidence of the struggles endured by those who had lived in this region from prehistoric times, viewers now saw on this monitor flashes of modern-history-in-the-making. That video montage called viewers to attend to a different kind of story—the struggle of the human spirit for freedom and the violence that has attended that struggle.

For pastors, congregational leaders, and worship teams seeking to understand how to incorporate media into a worship space in ways that communicate, as well as that call people to participate actively in contemplation, museums such as this one in Tralee offer important lessons. The entire museum experience was designed to tell a story, to stimulate our imaginations, to set our minds off to travel across time and space, and to engage our hearts and souls. Media art, just one element of this total multisensory, multi-arts experience, played its part well throughout the encounter. It was always appropriate and, aesthetically, of high quality. Carefully integrated wherever it was in place, the media projection itself was a work of art that invited us to entertain new insights. It was revelatory. It was designed so that visitors could "see." We were their first concern, because if what the media and graphic designers created did not communicate to us, if it did not speak to our minds and hearts, all their efforts would have been for naught.

In liturgy, worship and the people who worship must come first. All elements within the worship space need to work in concert to serve that priority. "The body of Christ gathered in prayer hallows the space used for worship" (principle S-4), not the degree to which a worship space is "high tech" or includes media art.

> The worship of the assembly, rather than architectural or artistic expression, creates sacred space. Architecture, furnishings, works of art, liturgical vessels, and other elements of the rites reach their noblest aim when they facilitate the sacred celebration of the people gathered for worship. (application S-4D)

Those elements include media technology and media art.

Considerations of time and space

Having considered briefly an Ash Wednesday service, how might media art be integral to encouraging worshipers' active participation in other Lenten services, such as Taizé prayers around a cross, or some variation on the medieval Stations of the Cross or the monastic Tenebrae service? Good Friday services might include a service around the seven last words of Jesus or a reader's theatre–style proclamation of the passion narrative from John's gospel.

Media art might be incorporated into of any of these Lenten services. In one Roman Catholic parish in Oregon, different groups took responsibility during Lent for creating media art for each week's Stations of the Cross. A youth group chose to accompany each station with an image of social injustice in the world. In "Digital Glass," a media-for-worship DVD collection from Sally Morgenthaler's

Sacramentis.com Web site, a three-and-a-half-minute video entitled "Stations" features stark, black-and-white abstract paintings of Christ's agonizing journey to Calvary. It can run silently, with or without text, with or without the accompanying contemporary pop song, "Lamb of God" by Twila Paris. Morgenthaler provides a variety of suggestions for how this media art might be used in a Lenten service. A parish might likewise commission a local photographer, visual artist, or media artist to create media art specifically for Lenten meditation that might be introduced on Ash Wednesday or the first Sunday in Lent. Each week thereafter, new elements might be added to the media art, or another artist's work might be offered for worshipers' reflection.

Where might this media art be located in the worship space, as well as within the flow of worship itself? As at the Kerry Museum, people might encounter media art on their way into a service, on their way out, or in multiple places throughout the liturgy. TV monitors might be nestled in a gathering space or narthex. Images might be projected on upper side walls, even ceilings. In thinking about how to integrate media art into worship, planning groups need to think *temporally*, across time—the entire liturgy or liturgical season—and *spatially*, throughout the entire worship space, which includes whatever spaces people encounter from parking lot to altar. They need to appreciate all the dimensions of time and space that contribute to people's experience of worship. This focus might be a challenge to some leaders' imaginations, because many planners find it easier to focus on the words or songs of a service. But thinking temporally and spatially is important in the liturgically appropriate integration of media into worship. Such reflection contributes to whether media in worship do or do not have the potential to serve liturgy as a moving word.

The media art in that Kerry Museum provided beauty from the very start, and that beauty opened up my heart so that by the end of the exhibit I was able to see and to contemplate even painful beauty, a people fighting for freedom. Its designers incorporated a variety of sights, sounds, and media. From first to last room, every element encountered in that space—varieties of media art among them—built upon the last. Together all of these carefully integrated artistic elements told a story of the life, death, and resurrection of a people. We, too, are charged with the awesome responsibility of preparing liturgies and working with our worship spaces in ways that help communicate the story of life, death, and resurrection we call paschal mystery. In telling our story, should we do any less?

For reflection and discussion

1. How do you react differently to media art that is in color and media art that is in black-and-white? Why?

2. As the sound of the *shofar* is the sound of the Jewish High Holy Days, what is the sound of Lent for you? What are the images of Lent? If you were to share them with a media artist who was charged with creating something for this coming Lent, what would you say?

3. In what circumstances have you experienced media art integrated within an event, such as the celebration of a public occasion or visit to a museum? How was that media art integrated? Did it stand out? Did it dominate? Did it blend in? Did it contribute?

4. What is your earliest memory of Lent? If a teen in your parish were to ask you to share it with others on camera, would you?

5. Lent is a time for almsgiving. What ministries in your congregation or organizations in your community would benefit from being the focus of a short documentary for Lenten worship? How might this media art move people to support these ministries financially or to volunteer their time? What would it take for media to make such a difference?

4
This Is the Night

The Vigil of Easter is an awesome event. If your parish has yet to discover this liturgical treasure, you might want to pull out your liturgical resources and lectionary and have a look at what is involved. When fully and joyously celebrated by a community, this ancient liturgy allows the primal symbols of fire and water to "speak" to our hearts anew and stimulates our religious imaginations through powerful storytelling and lavish ritual action.

Weather permitting, we begin outside beneath the stars around the dancing flames of a crackling fire. Literally ignited by that new fire, we set forth to be further enlightened by the word. Story after story of God's fierce, unfailing, faithful love overflows from a torrent of Old Testament readings, psalms, and poetry and from an amazing New Testament report of the confusing, even terrifying, news, "He is alive!" With our hearts on fire and imaginations filled to the brim, we dive directly into the life-giving waters of baptism. We arise wet from the font and glistening from blessed oil and go to dine at the banquet table of the risen Lord.

Easter Vigil is a marvelously multisensory celebration that, when planned and enacted with great care and creativity, can offer parishioners a potentially life-changing experience of raucous rejoicing and unbridled joy. Upon departing from Easter Vigils that have taken advantage of the great diversity of music available, Vigils during which pastors have made lavish use of the church's primal symbols and worshipers have taken active parts, people are often amazed at what time it is. They testify that time seems to have flown—even though the service they attended may have run two hours or more! They have been wrapped up in an experience of time-out-of-time, *kairos* time.

Some congregations have experimented with incorporating media art within their Easter Vigils. The creation story (Gen. 1:1—2:4a) often is the first reading they target for possible visual enhancement. The temptation is to make too literal the matching of images and words. Many vendors sell stock photographs and film footage of nature imagery, such as majestic mountains, flowing streams, racing clouds, sunrises and sunsets, and ocean waves crashing. This stock photography and film footage is of high quality, beautifully shot. It is the work of professional photographers and cinematographers. Depending on how it is incorporated into worship, though, it may serve only as a visual cliché. It might be shown during the proclamation of the creation story with its refrain, "And God saw that it was good." But if that footage is used in a lock-step fashion—scripture passage on light, images of the sun; scripture passage on creatures of the sea, images of sea creatures; scripture passage on four-legged creatures, images of four-legged animals—this media art might add little life to the proclamation of that passage. Of course, such media art may provide beauty if it is beautiful footage, but it may not function metaphorically to invite us to come to new insight. I advise, instead, attempting the art of juxtaposition.

Of juxtapositions in worship Gordon Lathrop has noted, "Meaning occurs through structure, by one thing set next to another" (*Holy Things: A Liturgical Theology*, 1993, p. 33). In working with sight, sound, and motion to produce media art, juxtaposition also functions in a revelatory way. When we set side by side images, words, and sounds that are not normally found together, we can produce media art that invites people in, because they need to interpret it. They need to wrestle with this art. In their effort they may find new meaning emerges. Rather than treating the creation story as though it were a documentary requiring word-and-image correspondence, then, church members might use the art of juxtaposition. They might marry unexpected imagery to this well-known passage so that it may be encountered again for the first time.

For Easter Vigil, we might turn for help to artists within our own community who are skilled in the art of juxtaposition—graphic designers, painters, collage artists—to illustrate this well-known story. Other media-savvy folk could then convert these original images into photo or digital formats for projection. In a worship space with mostly blank walls, film slide projectors might be set up in a variety of locations within the space so that images could appear and remain as illuminations on different walls. By the end of the reading, multiple images might surround the listening community that has been sitting in semidarkness.

Some congregations actually choose a space other than their sanctuary for the proclamation of the story of creation and other lectionary passages assigned for the Easter Vigil. Coming inside from the fire lighting, they may move into a fellowship hall or other flexible space where chairs might encircle the newly lighted paschal candle. This kind of space may provide the possibility for hanging materials onto which images could be projected.

Consider just a few other possibilities. Rather than have a changing series of images accompany Genesis 1, stunning video footage or a single image of star fields or galaxies might be played throughout the passage. Gazing at the heavens typically moves us to awe and wonder. This kind of attitude is apropos when listening to the creation story. Using this video as environmental media art could enhance worshipers' impression that they are sitting around a fire, beneath the stars, listening to a tribal retelling of their origins. Of course copyright permission needs to be secured for showing commercial footage, and fine options exist for those who wish to make the effort to secure permission. The wide-screen DVD collection *Baraka* contains beautiful footage of rotating star fields (www.mpi homevideo.com) and the DVD *Stargaze II: Visions of the Universe* (www.alphadvd.com) offers twelve clips of galaxies as seen through telescopes, including the Hubble telescope. Another approach to setting the stage for the creation story might be to use the opening scene from the film *Contact* (Warner Bros., 1997) as a prelude to the reading. That sequence carries us back in time to the big bang. These DVDs are available from a variety of online stores.

Following the story of the testing of Abraham (Gen. 22:1-18) is Psalm 16. Its antiphon, "You will show me the path of life," could be accompanied by a single image of a shopper making her way down a grocery aisle, with food on one side and books on another, or some other image that portrays everyday choice-making. Many such photographs, some copyright free, are available from Web sites. Alternately, local photographers or artists could provide their own interpretation for worshipers' contemplation during this psalm. Any time we can call upon the artists in our midst to offer their gifts to the church can be an occasion for joy for them and for the rest of us. As *Principles for Worship* rightly notes: "Original, commissioned artwork can reflect the worship life of a particular congregation. Artists can be nurtured and encouraged in their communities by the incorporation of their art in the worship life of the church" (application S-20E).

As an alternative to still photography, video footage could also be run in the background to accompany this psalm. An intergenerational production team of parishioners—teens, young adults, and older adults who together have basic skills in media production and theological reflection—could take on the challenge of interpreting this psalm. Discussing their differing locations on life's path might lead participants to share some rich realizations. Scripture commentaries and lectionary resources might spark team members' imaginations. For example, Gail Ramshaw's book, *Treasures Old and New: Images in the Lectionary* (2002) provides quotations, poetry, and her own reflections on the image of "Journey" that might stimulate much discussion. Ramshaw's *Words Around the Fire* (1990) also provides beautifully poetic reflections on the Easter Vigil scriptures that might stir parishioners to be likewise poetic in their approach to liturgical media art for this most important of nights in the Christian calendar.

Another Easter Vigil reading ripe for media art interpretation is the call of Jonah (Jonah 1:1—2:1). Early Christians often used the image of Jonah to refer to Jesus' resurrection. The third-century series of marble statuettes depicting the Jonah story found on the Cleveland Museum of Art's Web site (www.clevelandart.org/byzantine/curator.html) could inspire local artists to create their own twenty-first-century media art version of the Old Testament tale. Because it is a Bible story that often delights children, perhaps a Sunday school class might hear the story of the call of Jonah in the months before Easter and create their own art that could be animated to accompany this proclamation.

Art lovers—teachers and historians—possess a wealth of knowledge about art through the ages and art of diverse cultures, East and West. A worship team looking for art appropriate for Easter Vigil would no doubt greatly benefit from their knowledge. Most of the Easter Vigil Old Testament readings—the flood (Gen. 7:1-5, 11-18; 8:6-18; 9:8-13), the testing of Abraham (Gen. 22:1-18), the deliverance at the Red Sea (Exod.14:10-31; 15:20-21), the valley of the dry bones (Ezek. 37:1-14), and the deliverance of the three young men from the fiery furnace (Dan. 3:1-29)—have inspired many artists to create evocative works. With the permission of the copyright holders of these images, a single image of a work of art might be projected during a reading. (Since the art belongs to the nation, U.S. citizens are free to photograph whatever art they wish at the National Gallery of Art in Washington, D.C., as long as they do not use a flash.) I do not recommend producing a series of different artists' images for each reading, because a jumble of different art styles and periods might lack aesthetically necessary visual continuity. It might be visually jarring and distract worshipers from actually listening to the reading. But a single, worthy image might deepen worshipers' engagement with the word proclaimed. Perhaps a local art museum owns artwork depicting one of these stories and would lend or would permit a church to project a slide of that image. Certainly the work of modern Jewish artists, such as Marc Chagall, and that of contemporary Jewish painters and illustrators might provide just the right image to bring a new dimension to one of these important passages from the Hebrew scriptures. Education directors at Jewish museums might welcome the opportunity to introduce Christians to Jewish art.

Reaching out to the local art community can be an enriching experience. Each week in the 1970s Roman Catholic parishioners who celebrated what came to be called Liturgy in Santa Fe benefited from such collaboration. Volunteers sought out the work of local artists or borrowed art of all styles from local galleries and museums that was appropriate for the feast being celebrated or for the scripture being proclaimed. They displayed this two-dimensional and three-dimensional art in an attractive gallery-like entry space through which worshipers passed on their way to eucharist in their adobe chapel. Within the liturgy itself, they also incorporated and projected on a front wall of their chapel the work of local photographers and reproductions of religious art. Today this model of community outreach and cooperation could likewise be developed and could be a valuable aspect of a parish's evangelization efforts. Although I am mentioning ways media art might enhance or enrich the liturgy itself, I also urge congregations to connect with local artists who work in other media and to feature their art within their church buildings throughout the year.

Sundays and Seasons, an annual worship planning resource from Augsburg Fortress, provides much inspiration for those who wish to celebrate Easter Vigil. You will find listed on its pages all the possible readings as well as suggestions for music and worship environment. I do not recommend, however, that every reading receive media art accompaniment. Just as diversity in music styles is preferable for the Vigil, diversity in how media are employed is desirable, as well. Better to have less media art that is well done and totally appropriate for a few readings than to overreach and to try to deal with every reading. Given that each reading itself sounds a different narrative "tone," accompanying media art should respect that tone and, consequently, vary in style, treatment, and color range in ways appropriate to each reading.

"But I can't see . . . "

After the service of readings at the Easter Vigil, one or more baptisms may occur. However, a problem often confronts the worshipers who wish to witness and to affirm their support for the baptized. Except for those people nearest the font, many people cannot see any ritual action. If enough water is poured or splashed during the baptismal rite, people might be able to hear water being splashed or poured. Not much else of the baptismal action might be accessible. One way of handling the human desire to be up close and to see the action is to employ image magnification, also called IMAG. Lutheran churches have come to different ways of using this production technique in worship. The technique involves the recording of live action that is projected simultaneously onto large media screens.

Influenced by the practices of an Ohio megachurch and its ministers' use of image magnification for their seeker-oriented services, the pastor at a 200-member Lutheran church adopted image magnification in his community's services. Why would a small church choose this approach? For the benefit of worshipers seated in the back of their space, reported Pastor Kent Wilson. Each Sunday, when the children gathered at the front of the church to hear an age-appropriate message, a volunteer would use a video camera to capture what was happening on the floor in front of the pews. Another volunteer provided a cover shot of the service from a camera position in the back balcony. Image magnification was used at various points during the service with projected images being selected from either camera. After the first time image magnification was used for the children's message, church elders told the pastor they appreciated being able to see, for the first time, what was going on.

Worship leaders at Prince of Peace Lutheran Church in Burnsville, Minnesota—a community of 3,500 families whose worship space is outfitted with six media screens—use IMAG, as well, but differently. The pastoral staff made a conscious decision not to use this technique to "magnify" preachers or presiders but only to support worshipers' seeing something the preacher might be using as a prop or some important liturgical action occurring, such as a baptism. Early on in their use of image magnification, explains director of worship arts, Handt Hanson, they recognized that power issues are implicit when large projected live images of speakers or musicians loom over an assembly of any kind. The bigger the image, the greater the potential impact on the viewers and the greater the possibility of unethical manipulation of worshipers.

Some churches that offer seeker-friendly services or that are influenced by praise and worship-style services, use image magnification similarly to the way it is used for major addresses at conventions, conference lectures, and large-scale music concerts. Church leaders see IMAG as simply part of their overall communications efforts. This media production approach logically flows from a marketing model of evangelization, as well as from an education model of "preaching is teaching." The reasoning runs like this: if in our media culture people are used to high media production values and techniques such as IMAG, then the gospel must be packaged in ways attractive to this media-savvy crowd.

The leaders of congregations who have used IMAG know that this production technique can significantly affect worshipers' experience of a service and can create a particular kind of atmosphere within a worship space. It can make a service feel to those in attendance like a lecture experience or an entertainment experience. Although this technique surely may enrich and enhance oral communication, it certainly may also function in undesirable ways. Especially when a director is integrating live shots from multiple cameras, the media may highlight people in a way that makes them seem like celebrities and that enhances their image as stars.

Image magnification is commonly used in seeker services, because these services generally follow a performance model. These services typically emphasize the ministers and musicians on the stage. Ministers expect little participation from the people seated in the auditorium. In contrast, Lutheran liturgy assumes a participation model in which the assembly is expected to perform the liturgy: to be full, conscious, and active participants—not simply spectators. "Whenever we baptize, the image of the one being baptized is projected so that every one of the 1,300 people can see the [person's] face and the ritual in its fullness," notes Handt Hanson of Prince of Peace. "It does bring the worshiper into the ritual in an entirely new way." IMAG, then, can help people to participate more fully and consciously in a liturgical action that specifically calls for their active engagement as witnesses and as a community promising its support for the child or adult being baptized.

"When I was baptized . . . "

Another kind of media art might be appropriate following the celebration of the Easter Vigil. Footage of baptisms might be shared with parishioners on Easter morning or on subsequent Sundays. Parish producers might also consider doing interviews with people who were baptized or whose children were baptized at the Vigil. Well-edited, short video segments of people speaking about their liturgical experiences is a twenty-first–century approach to mystagogy, that is, reflection after a ritual on the grace experienced during it and since. During the weeks following Easter through to Pentecost Sunday, a short mystagogical video reflection could each week feature one of the baptized, a parishioner who experienced the baptism of a loved one, a new member of the congregation, or a teen who affirmed his or her baptism at confirmation. The reflections might be shown to the congregation as part of the opening rites, before the assembly remembers its own baptismal vows, or after communion.

Once into the Easter season, we are experiencing longer days. In an auditorium-style church with no or shaded windows, showing media art is not impeded by sunlight. However, in worship spaces with windows and significant ambient light, the incorporation of media art of any kind will require media screens made for daylight circumstances, video projectors powerful enough to display clear images despite sunlight, or video monitors located in darker areas of the church.

To use or not to use

To use media art or not to use media art; that is always the question we must address. Using today's media of any kind in our liturgies is not a given. It is a choice. Even if chosen, media art need not be integrated every week. I realize that some church people, having experienced media in worship, cannot imagine liturgy without it. I interviewed parishioners at a Roman Catholic church in Cincinnati who, since 1977, had celebrated liturgy every Sunday with projected media art above the altar. Their media art, though, was a single image held throughout a section of the liturgy as well as a post-communion slide-based media meditation with live song. They saw their "AV," as they called it, as their version of stained glass since their worship space had no windows. Parishioners in their 30s who had grown up with this approach to media art in liturgy missed it terribly when they moved elsewhere. (For more on my field research, see *Testing the Fruits: Aesthetics as Applied to Liturgical Media Art*, noted in the resource list.) After extensive exposure, people in churches Protestant and Catholic where lyrics, prayers, scripture, and announcements have been projected weekly likewise may find the prospect of a media-less liturgy less than desirable. It might be as unthinkable as a Lutheran service without congregational singing. But as I close this chapter I do wish to make clear that *no* liturgy has to have media technology or media art incorporated into it. It is an option to be chosen with great care and to be executed with ongoing discernment, prayer, and attention.

Sustained use of media in worship requires the recruitment, training (liturgical, scriptural, technical, and aesthetic), and ongoing spiritual formation of many people, most of whom may be volunteers. Without a congregation's commitment to regular recruitment of "new blood," training, and formation, and without constant evaluation of how media art does or does not serve their liturgy, media ministers can burn out and media in worship can become hackneyed, clichéd, slap-dash, or shallow. As with other aspects of parish life, "choices in its use of money, property, and other resources reflect a community's commitment to service and ministry" (principle S-24). When faced with the choice of investing in the training and formation of people who could contribute to Communal Co-creation and to a parish's media ministry or of buying the latest and greatest media equipment or software, I would opt for the people. Without them, their spiritual insights, their growing technical skills, their aesthetic formation, and their lively imaginations, there is no media ministry. Of what use is having the latest technology if the people using it have no vision?

For reflection and discussion

1. Read one of the Old Testament lessons for Easter Vigil. What images or actions jump out at you? What metaphors might you want to engage if you were to develop media art for that liturgy?

2. What connections has your congregation made with the arts community in your area? How might connections be fostered in the years to come?

3. What experience of IMAG have you had? What was the effect of this production technique on you? Did you find yourself watching the screens more than the live action itself? Or did it make those on stage seem more present for you?

4. Is it really necessary for people to see the action of baptisms? If so, why? If not, why not?

5. What local resources might your congregation tap for the ongoing training and formation of volunteers who might enter your media ministry? How could you go about discovering who might be available?

5
How Long, O God?

The place: a darkened conference room. The occasion: an ecumenical gathering of Christians who have come together for a service of intercession for the world. The time: night. The season: whenever people are suffering (i.e., any time). Participants gather to close their days of discussion with prayer. As they enter the space, they discover the room is illuminated by the flickering light of many video monitors. Ten or so monitors encircle the space, a kind of technological Stonehenge. As they arrive, the participants can hear the sounds of many languages being spoken at the same time. They see on the monitors the recognizable format of news programs. As they move into the space, they come to take their place in the circular arrangement of chairs. In the center, a tall paschal candle stands. Its single flame dances. Via video, participants can see and hear the news of the day as it has been broadcast in Korean, Japanese, Spanish, French, German, Serbian, Russian, Chinese, Igbo, Arabic, English. Amidst the babble of languages and the display of video footage, viewers can see and hear the images and sounds of human and ecological suffering: earthquakes, famine, flood, war, violence, murder, poverty, disease, hurricanes and typhoons, politics, and power. The stuff of daily news. These realities cannot be missed, even though viewers do not understand the languages of most of these news reports.

As the sounds of the news readers and reporters fade, the night prayer begins. Participants are invited to add their sung "Kyrie eleison" to a multilingual litany. They sing for some time, "Lord, have mercy." As they do, the TV images continue to call for their contemplation. In an audio "cross-fade," the sounds of the world increase in volume as the chant decrescendos and comes to an end. The voice of a prayer leader speaks of the suffering of the world and calls upon the God of compassion to show mercy and to teach humanity the ways of mercy and compassion. She invites the participants to meditate upon a world in need. The participants are now free to remain seated, to gather around a single video monitor to view its stories, or to walk around the room viewing the many stories as they unfold upon the screens. The sounds of the world's latest tragedies once again fill the space.

After many minutes of people's silent meditation, of people looking and listening to these reports, the volume of the reports once again decreases enough for all to hear a leader of prayer call those present to stand in solidarity with the suffering peoples of the earth and to offer prayers for the world. After each petition, the person raising up the prayer and others likewise sharing in that petition, move to the center of the prayer space, take up a taper, and light it from the paschal candle. The petitioners bring their candles to the monitor whose imagery has called them to prayer and place the lit taper in a sand-filled container, one of which is located near each monitor. Prayers can be spoken or enacted or both.

As the prayers continue, the growing number of lighted candles increases the overall illumination of the space, as happens during an evening prayer *lucernarium* or the Easter Vigil. The service eventually closes with a prayer to "Our Father and Mother . . . your will be done. . . . Give us today. . . . Save us from the time of trial and deliver us from evil." As this pleading fills the space, the cacophonous sounds of the news reports rise once more. Then the sound stops, the screens go to black, and all that illumines the space are the candles. A sign of what? Worshipers are left to come to their own conclusions. A prayer leader offers a closing benediction and dismissal to "go forth and serve the suffering of the world." As their first response to that command, the participants offer each other a sign of peace.

Most people who have experienced the use of media in worship have the impression that the only way to use it is projected upon huge media screens located at center or to both or either side of a stage or altar area. But, as the examples in the previous chapters have suggested, this model is only one option, and may not even be the best option for a particular worship service. Much depends on the community, the worship, the space, the time, and the circumstances in which media are elements of worship.

Video artists, media artists, and video installation artists have other ideas about how media hardware and software can be used to produce an experience that allows us to move beyond the usual boundaries of our perception of the world. We have much to learn from these artists. Video artists have insisted that broadcast television is not the only way this medium can be channeled, that video is a language, not a commodity or a piece of furniture. Independent outsiders, these artists often use video to critique television, to challenge commercialization of our culture, to spotlight instances of commodification of life, and to address the meaning and experience of time. (See Doug Hall and Sally Jo Fifer, *Illuminating Video: An Essential Guide to Video Art*, 1990.) Since the mid-1960s, media artists working in "projective imagery" have experimented with projection of still and moving images on different kinds of surfaces, through translucent materials, upon multiple walls, and in unexpected contexts. (See Chrissie Iles, *Into the Light: The Projected*

Image in American Art 1964–1977, 2001.) Installation artists Tony Oursler, Nam June Paik, and Bill Viola are among American artists who have accomplished in their own artworks what *Principles for Worship* describes as the "ongoing challenge for planners of the house of the church": working in and with "creative tension" that "calls for deliberate efforts to express the timeless in a timely fashion" (application S-5E). To encounter the work of these artists is to grapple with mystery. (For an introduction to the great diversity of installation art, see Nicholas de Oliveira, Nicola Oxley, and Michael Petry, *Installation Art* [1994]. For a historical treatment of this art, see Julie H. Reiss, *From Margin to Center: The Spaces of Installation Art* [1999].) I do not always like, and know I do not always appreciate, their work or that of other video, media, and installation artists. Some media artists play so much with my perception that I find myself experiencing vertigo. I have a variety of reactions to media art. Some works amuse, some confuse, some confound, and some even disgust me. But each time I have wrestled with video, media, and installation art in museums, art galleries, and churches, I have had no choice but to actively participate in it. I have had to ask myself, "What is going on? What does this mean?" I have been drawn into contemplation and meaning-making.

Bill Viola intentionally creates media installations that invite viewers to address issues of life, death, and resurrection. I have experienced his work in the Episcopal Cathedral of St. John the Divine, as well as in museums in New York City (www.billviola.com). Tony Oursler projects video onto unexpected surfaces and materials in multimedia assemblages that often explore the human suffering associated with isolation, loneliness, and deep anxiety and despair (www.tonyoursler.com). Nam June Paik's approach to creating an environment that unexpectedly incorporates media with plants and other objects inspired, in part, the liturgical example that opened this chapter (www.paikstudios.com). But inspiration can come from encounters outside of museums and galleries, such as a chance encounter that long ago fired my imagination. On a visit to the Eiffel Tower in Paris, I decided I really did not need to go to the highest level to see the view and instead explored a lower level of this structure. There I discovered an entire floor full of TV monitors displaying live broadcasts of television programs from nations around the globe. So deeply affected by an experience of feeling surrounded by the voices of the world, I was moved to pray.

I invite you to explore this whole area of video, media, and installation art, because the way media technology and media art are currently used in most worship services is not essentially different from the way they were used in the mid-1960s and 1970s. It is just that the equipment is digital rather than analog, and much more expensive. The insights of contemporary media artists have not entered our worship, except in a limited way through young people who have been creating since the mid-1990s an approach to communal prayer known as "alternative worship," a topic addressed in the next chapter. This situation is a shame, because, as in the past, the church needs today's artists to help us see again for the first time the mystery that is the life God has entrusted to us. We have barely tapped that potential. What might we learn if we were to invite artists to help us create media art for worship? We might learn anew about the value of "creative tension" and about how to make and select media that are open-ended, metaphorical, and poetic so that they might crack open a space in hardened hearts through which the Spirit might speak.

Rest eternal grant, O Lord

The mystery of one aspect of life—suffering—is directly confronted when communities prepare for and hold funerals, liturgies of healing, and liturgies of lament. Media art may find a place in such liturgies. In the case of funerals, it already has. In two parishes I have studied in Oregon and Ohio, loved ones of someone who has died have the option to bring to the church a selection of images of the deceased. Families usually are grateful to have this option and take it. A volunteer or someone on the staff scans these images and edits them into a media meditation that is shown either during a prelude or after communion. At a church in Minnesota, a family member of a deceased parishioner created his own video disc montage of images and brought it to the pastor so that she could incorporate it into the funeral liturgy. A United Methodist pastor in Arizona, Jeff Procter-Murphy, conducted a straightforward video interview with one of his parishioners two weeks before she died of cancer. She wanted some way to communicate one last affirmation of the gift of life to her high school students. The pastor showed a two-and-a-half-minute video clip edited from their conversation during the teacher's memorial service, which was attended by more than 300 people, mostly teenagers.

Heal us, O Lord

Liturgies of healing offer another opportunity for media to serve liturgy. An order of healing may be incorporated with holy communion or a service of the word following the hymn of the day. At various points within this particular kind of service, media art might be appropriate if it is sensitively produced and placed within the overall movement of this liturgy. A starting point might simply be the projection of images from scripture stories of healing that serve as environmental art when people enter the worship space. During this time, flashy special effects, jazzy transitions, and quick-cut editing would likely be inappropriate to the tone and mood of the service. Consider, for example, this opening address from the order for healing to be included in the ELCA's new core worship resource, *Evangelical Lutheran Worship*:

> Our Lord Jesus healed many as a sign of God come near,
> and sent the disciples to continue this work of healing—
> with prayer, the laying on of hands, and anointing.

In the name of Christ,
  the great healer and reconciler of the world,
we now entrust to God all who are in need of healing.

Images representing the healing of the paralytic were among the artwork found on the walls of the baptismal space in the oldest extant Christian house church, the third-century Roman outpost of Dura-Europa in Eastern Syria. The artwork is simply sketched, the work of a local amateur artist perhaps. We see two scenes: a man on a cot-like bed, and that same man with that bed hoisted over his shoulder. A third-century fresco in the Roman catacomb of Sts. Peter and Marcellino features a simple depiction of Jesus healing the woman with a hemorrhage. Artists have depicted these and other healing stories on ancient sarcophagi reliefs, the pages of illuminated manuscripts, Byzantine icons and mosaics, Western medieval church door reliefs and stained glass, and religious paintings of more recent centuries.

In imagining this possibility, my liturgist and media-producer intuition and training cry for caution. During Internet searches to see what kinds of images have been created on the theme of Jesus' healing, I was struck that the style and color palette of any images displayed or projected during a liturgy of healing should not be in the style of the highly colored dramatic and emotion-filled Renaissance paintings or of modern-day sentimental illustrations of Bible stories. Rather, media art attuned to the liturgy would be art that exhibits a style that is more reserved, spare, or iconic.

A liturgy of healing is not the time to introduce dramatic, intense scenes of healing, whether from paintings or feature films. The people most likely to attend healing services typically come to gain some measure of peace, a healing touch, a sense of being cared for and loved by the body of Christ. The point of incorporating any images at all is not to raise their expectations of being cured, but to support their trust in a God who can bring healing of many kinds, even if not physical healing at that moment. Great care must be taken to avoid improper manipulation of people's emotions through the inept or insensitive selection of media art integrated into the service. People who are ill already feel vulnerable. They should be treated with great tenderness, respect, and empathy. Why not, in planning for the service, consult with them about images, psalms, songs, or stories they associate with healing, or music that gives them hope? Parish nurses and clinical social workers would be good consultants for a worship team that was thinking through how media art might help to create a healing environment, one that would reflect the theology of the closing prayer from the healing liturgy proposed in *Life Passages: Marriage, Healing, Funeral*:

> God of mercy, source of all healing,
> we give thanks for your gifts of strength and life,
> and especially for your Son, Jesus Christ,
> the health and salvation of the world.
> Help us by your Holy Spirit
> to feel your power in our lives
> and to know your eternal love;
> through Christ our Lord. Amen.
> (Renewing Worship, vol. 4, 2002, p. 30)

Other moments in a liturgy of healing during which media art might be helpful could be times of instrumental music or chant. Often, Taizé chants are sung during the laying on of hands, while people are being anointed. During this liturgical action, artful extreme close-up photographs of hands touching other hands or of glistening oil might serve the moment. Single images might accompany congregational singing of songs such as "Healer of our every ill" or the spiritual "There is a balm in Gilead." A newer hymn that might inspire media art is the poignant "When memory fades and recognition falters" (*Renewing Worship Songbook*, R 270). Janet Walton offers poignant vignette-style examples of multisensory, multi-art liturgies of healing in *Feminist Liturgy: A Matter of Justice* (2000). Mari West Zimmerman has written another helpful resource, *Take and Make Holy: Honoring the Sacred in the Healing Journey of Abuse Survivors* (1995), that provides models for various types of healing liturgies.

Why, O God?

Each year, many communities search for ways to create services for World AIDS Day. Some incorporate video to hear again the voices and see again the faces of those who have died. Others choose to show documentary footage of those suffering from HIV/AIDS around the world, including the little ones left orphaned by the thousands. On other occasions, painful communal situations or events might lead a parish or parish group to decide to offer a liturgy of lament.

The Bible contains many powerful psalms of lament, but most churches have not explored how to bring lamentation into worship, despite the fact that people may need to express this intense emotion. J. Frank Henderson has developed a collection entitled *Liturgies of Lament* (1994) that provides models for liturgies in memory of the holocaust, the bombing of Hiroshima and Nagasaki, violence against creation, and violence against individuals or groups. The ELCA's Web site contains prayers for times of natural disaster, such as hurricanes, tornados, fires, and floods (www.elca.org/disaster/resources). Within any of these liturgies media art might be integrated, such as historical footage or the videotaped testimony of victims. *Renewing Worship Songbook* contains a section devoted to the topic of lament. Among its fine offerings are "In deepest night" (R 235) and "How long, O God" (R 238) with Ralph Smith's powerful text of lament, hope, and trust in God. In working with these resources, a community may see ways to use media art as an element integral to the service, an interpretation of one of the psalms of lamentation, perhaps.

National tragedies can spur efforts to address in worship the issue of suffering and the searing question, "Why, O God?" After Hurricane Katrina devastated New Orleans and much of the Gulf Coast and Florida in 2005, The Work of the People production group produced a series of interviews, a documentary, and other video clips for use in worship. After the terrorist attacks of September 11, 2001, every congregation scrambled to develop liturgies that could somehow address that national trauma. Whatever media art some churches had planned for the following Sunday had to be scrapped and other media quickly produced . . . or not. Since the events of September 11, I have seen a troubling trend on some media-for-worship Web sites of the visual equating of American flags with the cross and other images and video that feed into an "Our God is better than your God" form of American nationalism. Such triumphalistic media art is inappropriate for Christian worship, just as national flags are best left outside the doors of our worship spaces. As *Principles for Worship* advises: "Flags signal national loyalties and may become divisive, implying that a particular national identity is synonymous with the Christian way" (application S-16H).

Liturgies of lament are not only for times of illness, catastrophe, war, or national disaster. Faith communities facing suffering caused by some injustice, local or systemic, may want to develop a ritual opportunity for communal lament. Typically, such services call people to acknowledge and to confess their complicity in the perpetuation of injustice, to express their repentance, to seek God's strength to aid their conversion, and to ask for God's help to commit themselves to the way of justice for all peoples. Media artists, amateur and professional, would be of great help in creating the environment for liturgies of lament, for producing soul-searching documentaries and video testimonies, for capturing the face of injustice on film, and for providing a vision of what the way of justice might look and sound like in their community and in the world.

During funerals, liturgies of healing, or liturgies of lament, media art may serve well in many and various ways. Local worship planners and congregations know best their pain. Local media artists, especially young ones, might develop media art in a style I have rejected but that is appropriate for their circumstances. Regardless of what style may be chosen, the selection or production of media art for such times needs to be done with utmost care for those already suffering and for others who stand by feeling helpless in the face of pain and injustice.

For reflection and discussion

1. People bring photos of their deceased loved ones to funeral homes and place them near the coffin. How would incorporating such photographs within a funeral service in church be similar or different in how it might affect mourners?

2. What biblical stories of healing have brought you hope, comfort, or solace? What metaphors, images, or art would you use as the basis for media art for a liturgy of healing?

3. Think of times when your community has had to face a natural disaster or some other tragedy. A common instinct leads people to set up improvised shrines at a site of sudden loss. They may include photos, candles, flowers, stuffed animals, and other items symbolic of their grief and of solidarity with those who died and those who mourn. How might liturgical media art—perhaps even including images of the people's ritual shrine-building—provide another way to help a community grieve in worship?

4. How might biblical healing stories be illustrated today by someone in your parish or by a local media artist?

5. Sections of the AIDS Quilt traveled around the United States for many years. How might media art serve in liturgy as did the AIDS Quilt Project in many communities?

6. How might media art created for funerals or liturgies of healing or lament be reused in other church gatherings or on church Web sites? For what purposes?

7. In producing media art for worship, what would be your criteria for determining when it may become unethically manipulative of people's emotions?

6
Teach Us to Use Your Gifts Carefully . . . and Innovatively!

A storm blown across the prairie has drenched the college campus. Branches broken by the wind litter the quad. First-year students bundled in their hooded sweatshirts and windbreakers step on wet yellow and red leaves as they head down the concrete path. It's slippery going. Dusk arrives early these days. Night comes on fast. The first weeks of college seem to have raced by even faster. Already it is time for midterm exams. The all-nighters have begun. Anxious, the students arrive. Once through the doors, they discover video monitors illuminating the entry, stairway landings, and hallway as they descend to the chapel. Some students stand and watch the video monitors for a while. They see extreme close-up images of blazing autumn leaves that make this bit of creation seem like abstract art. On the monitor placed on one landing they encounter honking Canada geese silhouetted as they wing across a dusky sky. A bank of video monitors of different sizes stands at the entry to the chapel. On the screens flows aerial footage of fields empty of their harvest, row upon row, field after field.

In the chapel itself, the usual folding chairs have been stashed away to make room for rucksack pillows and bales of hay. As they perch themselves wherever they choose, most of the undergrads recognize the rhythmic sounds that fill the space. Harvesters. The sounds of machinery gradually fade until all present are enveloped in silence. Throughout the space flicker candles in glass Mason jars, safely out of harm's way. At one end of the space, a single wall-size image is projected. Tonight it is an extreme close-up black-and-white photograph of a crumpled piece of paper. Projected onto another wall are simple slides—white text and melody line on black background. They provide the opening chanted dialogue between the prayer leader and the assembly.

> The Lord almighty grant us a quiet night and peace at the last.
> **Amen.**
> It is good to give thanks to the Lord,
> **to sing praise to your name, O Most High;**
> to herald your love in the morning,
> **your truth at the close of the day.** (*LBW*, 154)

The seniors responsible for tonight's worship service know well the pressure of these first exams and papers. Many easily recall how homesick they felt as first-year students. All the excitement of football games is not enough to keep away the panic midterms can induce. They have decided to offer a midnight service every night during midterms. They have turned to the ancient form of night prayer called *compline*. It is a short service, twenty minutes at most. Each night the opening silence has grown deeper. Each night the students' voices have gained in strength as the first-year students have become confident of the chanted parts. Each night another single black-and-white image serves as a visual metaphor for the painful harvest they are trying to reap. The prayers connect with them: "You are in our midst, O Lord, and you have named us yours; do not forsake us, O Lord our God" (Jer. 14:9).

The ancient treasury of morning, evening, and night prayer awaits the discovery of young and old alike. These flexible forms of prayer provide a basic liturgical structure that can be adapted endlessly. How might media art provide a moving word in these services?

Environmentally. In the preceding scene, edited video footage of autumnal sights and sounds provided a hospitable greeting. Images welcomed worshipers. Sights and sounds led them to the worship space. The media art drew the harried students onward and called on them to attend and to begin to focus and to settle down. On this dark and stormy night, the warm colors of the media art—created by seniors skilled in videography—provided evidence of the haunting beauty of creation they could not see in the darkness, surely a cause for stirring praise.

Metaphorically. A single image—a crumpled piece of paper—met the students and introduced silently a metaphor that acknowledged the jumbled state they were in. The metaphor of harvest—of fields and academic effort—ran through the composed and extemporaneous prayers. Juxtaposed against each other, the wall-size photograph and one of the psalms assigned for night prayer spoke to fearful hearts.

> Answer me when I call, O God, defender of my cause;
> you set me free when I am hard-pressed;
> have mercy on me and hear my prayer. (Ps. 4:1, *LBW*)

The advantages of evening services

Services in darkness or semidarkness have advantages and disadvantages. For communities whose worship space in the day time is filled with radiant sunshine, evening or night becomes prime time for the possibility of including media art in worship. No need for expensive, powerful video projectors that can provide crisp projected images even in the daylight. Within a darkened space, less powerful, less expensive projectors will do. Even overhead projectors can serve well!

Depending on the worship space, its size and shape, and the number of people who will be attending a service, surfaces other than commercially purchased media screens might work. James Wetzstein, University Associate Pastor at Valparaiso University in Indiana, celebrates a Wednesday evening eucharist with students. Conducted in the small Gloria Christi Chapel, the service incorporates student-created media meditations that are projected on a faceted glass wall over which is draped the translucent lightweight material called scrim, a fabric used in scenery for theatre productions. Images can be projected from the front or from behind this fabric. He reports that the projected art is further enhanced by the faceted glass surface against which the fabric hangs. Each week an art student produces media art for this service.

The ability to change or rearrange a worship space, as in these college situations, is important: "Flexibility of space and portability of furniture facilitate the variations of worship as well as related activities of congregation and community" (principle S-19). And, as one of this principle's applications reminds us, "the ability to arrange the furnishings within the worship space in various ways gives a congregation the freedom to adapt as changes and new ideas are introduced" (application S-19C). The introduction of liturgical media art is one of those new ideas.

Projection options

To look at technology for worship trade magazines and promotional materials that are provided to the "houses of worship" market, a reader could get the impression that the only possible projection surfaces are screens like the large media screens that flank the stage at megachurches or large plasma screens located on front walls in a darkened side area of a smaller church. When appropriately sized for the worship space and the needs of the congregation, these screens do work well and provide crisp, sharp images that make text easy to read and that provide clear, colorful graphic reinforcement of the theme of a service. If a congregation decides to make the investment of incorporating media technology and media projection into their services, its leaders do need to work with qualified professionals who can help create a customized solution for maximum visibility of projected or displayed media. As *Principles for Worship* advises: "The effective use of media and technology often calls for particular skills and training" (application S-15A). However, not all congregations or communities need or are ready to make a commitment to investing in media technology and projection equipment. Where media art is being used to create a worship environment through color, sound, or movement, crisp, bright projected imagery might not be as critical a priority as in typical worship circumstances.

Alternative worship approaches to media art

The Church of the Apostles (COTA) in Seattle, Washington, is a good example of a community that experiments and improvises with media technology and media art and how both serve liturgy. This Lutheran-Episcopal church plant in the city center focuses on reaching out to young adults, the unchurched as well as the formerly churched (www.apostleschurch.org). Its Web site describes the community: "*CHURCH OF THE APOSTLES* is a *future church with an ancient faith* . . . in the story of jesus, we have glimpsed god's future and know that '*thiscouldchangeeverything.*'" The way the community uses media in worship reflects its ancient-future commitment to exploring and to retrieving the liturgical prayers, music, art, and spiritual practices of Christians throughout the ages and to proclaiming the gospel in ways appropriate to techno-savvy young people. Photographs on COTA's "community worship" Web page give some idea of how their worship is a multimedia, multisensory experience:

> in approach, apostles worship is neither "traditional" (50s) nor "contemporary" (60s–80s) but *ancient-future* (today). ancient-future worship speaks to postmodern generations and draws

equally upon ancient (hymns, chant, candles, communion) and techno-modern (alt. rock, art, ambient, projection, video) sources, so there is no need to 'check your culture at the door.' so, come as you are, wear your jeans, show your body art, tote your java, and be @ home spiritually, with god, and among friends.

Ryan Marsh, director of liturgical arts for COTA, possesses good liturgical sense and many skills for creating graphic art. Guided by founding ELCA pastor Karen Ward, he and other community members bring great creativity to planning worship services that may be held in the COTA tea house, a church building across the street they have recently purchased, or in rented spaces including warehouses or galleries they have used for special liturgies, such as Easter Vigil. During a phone interview, Ryan Marsh spoke animatedly about the many ways the COTA community is re-imagining worship for the twenty-first century.

For several years now, Marsh has been creating graphic art projected during worship that gives worship participants a sense for the liturgical season, provides prayer texts they might not know, supports a sermon, signals different sections of a liturgy, or invites them into meditation or some ritual action. His media art functions in all five ways introduced in Chapter 3:

- To encourage participation
- To convey information
- To reinforce and enrich oral communication
- To open up an interactive space—within or outside us— for discovery
- To provide beauty

His work varies widely stylistically from photo montages that incorporate religious art or Byzantine icons, to evocative photographs edited and reworked in Adobe Photoshop, to aesthetically elegant graphic designs with well-chosen type fonts for text. His graphic art is typical of postmodern pastiche art and may "sample" visual material from a variety of sources. I cannot include his images in this book, but I wish I could. They are so often simply beautiful. *Principles for Worship* suggests that "while definitions of beauty vary according to personal and cultural tastes, it is possible to identify some helpful criteria, such as balance and scale, color scheme, and quality materials honestly crafted" (application S-20D). I find all of these qualities in this young media artist's liturgical media art. Although Marsh is not a professional graphic designer, he is an amateur artist who strives to create something beautiful for God and the community. His work sometimes reflects the playfulness of a service, sometimes its deeply solemn mood.

Marsh and other members of the COTA community, like others who create "alternative worship," turn to many forms of art and technology and mix and match them in ways baby boomer leaders in other churches seldom do. For more information on alternative worship, including images, definitions, history, and worship orders, see www.alternativeworship.org and other alternative worship Web sites linked to this portal site. Groups who identify themselves as a part of this worship movement exist in Australia, Canada, Germany, New Zealand, Switzerland, the United Kingdom, and the United States. Two books that provide an introduction to the alternative worship approach to ritual, examples of services, and much food for thought are Mark Riddell, Mark Pierson, and Cathy Kirkpatrick, *The Prodigal Project: Journey into the Emerging Church* (2000), and Jonny Baker, Doug Gay, and Jenny Brown, *Alternative Worship: Resources from and for the Emerging Church* (2003).

The encouragement of participation is an important objective in planning worship and in designing performance, interactive media, and installation art. Interactivity is a feature of much alternative worship and of worship developed by some other Emerging Church communities. The media equipment or materials used to encourage interactivity can be low-tech to high-tech. Ryan Marsh, for example, bought four old overhead projectors from a school equipment surplus sale for $5 each. For one service, the COTA worship team placed a projector on each side of their altar and, during the prayers of the people, invited worshipers to write their prayers on the transparencies. These petitions were then immediately seen projected on the walls. During a service addressing how we listen to God, they set up a computer on which people could send an e-mail question to god@apostleschurch.org. By projecting each of these e-mails on a screen, all worshipers became participants in the experience. For Advent 2005, a local artist created on a six- by four-foot semitransparent piece of plastic (left by the previous owners of their church building) an outline of the Madonna and Child. She color-coded sections of the outline. Using colored markers assigned for particular sections of the image, worshipers wrote their prayers of hope onto this canvas. By Christmas, their prayers had colored this image and reflected four week's worth of petitions of the COTA community and guests.

A COTA worship service—whether a eucharist or evening prayer—might attract 60 to 100 people, whose ages range from their late 20s to early 30s (with a few folk in their 50s and 60s, as well). More and more college students are gradually being drawn to this lively, life-giving community. As a consequence, the worship planners consistently have to provide media art that will help that 30 percent or more of the congregation who never have worshiped at COTA before and who may never have even attended a Christian service. "We hope to facilitate divine encounters," Marsh explains. Sometimes those encounters are triggered by the unexpected, such as a variety of alarm clocks going off at the start of an Advent worship in response to the scriptural admonition, "Keep awake!" (Mark 13:37b). Marsh quips, "On occasion it is important for worship to be disruptive."

The COTA community frequently reaches out to the arts community of Seattle and invites artists' contributions to their worship. Worship planners also incorporate as environmental art purchased video that may be projected onto a thin light-colored cloth that separates their foyer area from the worship space itself. Sometimes media art is projected on most of the surrounding walls and envelopes the worshiping community with photographs, graphic art, abstract patterns, or video art keyed to the scripture texts or liturgical season.

Other small communities of young Christians have likewise been bringing all their artistic gifts and rich imaginations to creating a worthy, Spirit-filled, multisensory, multi-arts environment for prayer. I applaud their efforts and commend them to other congregations who are seeking ways to proclaim the word in new ways. Visit them whenever you get a chance. In planning for a new or renewed worship space, "visiting and experiencing the liturgy in other places of worship is valuable for all who are engaged in the process of designing liturgical spaces"—even if you are designing temporary spaces (application S-22B). Likewise, "people with training and experience in creating liturgical space are essential partners in renewed use of existing spaces and in new construction projects" (principle S-23).

These innovative communities are on to something important, especially as it pertains to liturgical art and to media art in worship. Not limited by already installed media screens in auditorium spaces, they are finding different ways of introducing media technology and art into their worship services in temporary spaces, as well as in Gothic-style worship spaces. They have been influenced, whether consciously or not, by video and media artists, installation artists, and performance artists who often incorporate media into their multi-arts works. They have benefited from insights coming from several decades of women collaboratively creating feminist liturgy. They have learned from the ecumenical Taizé and Iona communities. They can fashion their own rituals, but they also work within traditional orders of worship. They know that the text in a ritual book is only a starting point. They have to bring themselves and all of their gifts to worship. They understand worship to be a community effort, not the effort of a single pastor or parish staff.

Furthermore, their commitment to inclusion makes a strong connection between the work of worship and the work of justice. Justice issues are involved in the shaping of a community's space for prayer: "Worship space that reflects intentional consideration of the diversity of culture and ethnic background within the congregation and its surrounding community is one way of expressing a commitment to social justice" (application S-6E). An aspect of justice, as well as of hospitality, is intentional inclusiveness of people, art, and cultures represented in media art that communities purchase or create. "Christian hospitality is culturally inclusive and recognizes the rich diversity of God's people in dimensions such as gender, race, age, class, ethnic background, and ability. Giving attention to this diversity within the worship space invites the participation of all within the community and speaks to the unity of the body of Christ" (application S-17D).

Right now for liturgy in churches Lutheran, Episcopal, and Catholic, the available harvest of commercial and homegrown media art for worship is plenty, but too few are the harvesters who know how to separate the wheat from the chaff. The concept of "liturgical media art," that is, media art *of* worship not just in it, is a concept that I have been advancing and teaching for only the past five years. As we contemplate the future use of media in worship, perhaps we might offer this adapted prayer for harvest from *Lutheran Book of Worship*: "Teach us to use your gifts carefully, that our land, our lives, and our arts may continue to yield their increase, through our brother, Jesus Christ our Lord" (*LBW*, 39, adapted).

For reflection and discussion

1. To what degree are children, teens, and young adults active in planning for worship in your parish?

2. How might your youth program become an occasion for Communal Co-creation of liturgical media art? How might your community affirm the talents of these young people and encourage them to become media artists for your liturgies?

3. What is your church's attitude toward media technology and media art in worship? Suspicion? Enthusiasm? What is the basis for that attitude? Is it justified?

4. Look at the texts of the harvest hymn "We plow the fields and scatter" (LBW 362) and the evening hymn "All praise to thee, my God, this night" (LBW 278). What sounds and sights are triggered in your imagination? What scenes from movies or television programs come to mind?

5. In what ways might your community be able to improvise in your worship space? What flexibility of arrangement do you now have? How might you gain flexibility to accommodate not only those physically disabled but also to allow for the space to be adapted on occasion to suit the needs of liturgy? If your space is inflexible, what other space might you use when your current seating arrangement is unhelpful to the celebration of a particular liturgy?

7
For All the Saints

In preparation for the 2005 Churchwide Assembly of the Evangelical Lutheran Church in America in Orlando, Florida, planners invited every ELCA congregation to submit photographs of ministry in their communities. They received a wonderfully wide array of images. When participants arrived at the convention center for the opening liturgy, on two large media screens they saw more than 200 images of ELCA saints-in-ministry come marching into their assembly to join those physically assembled. What a beautiful sight! Via media art, opening music, and procession, ELCA members absent and present were symbolically gathered as the body of Christ.

Just imagine . . .
With advance thought and planning, the gathering of worshipers physically present and those unavoidably absent from parish, synod, or youth gatherings can be accomplished by using media technology and media art. Imagine what might be possible if churches set themselves the task of making worship truly accessible to all, something to which all might contribute, even those absent. Via cable,

satellite, microwave, or Internet technologies, people confined at home, living in institutions, or incarcerated in prisons could receive a live broadcast of worship, perhaps even from their home parish. Televised worship is a common form of one-way church communication. But what about two-way communication? How could people gathered for Sunday worship not only know they are connected with those receiving a live transmission of their service, but also experience the gifts of those people who are not physically present?

Let's play out this scenario. Say the year is 2015. Media production skills have become common in schools, and even middle school children can produce quality video footage, well framed and well lighted. Family or student media production teams could visit those parishioners unable to attend worship and, with their permission, interview them.

What kinds of topics might they discuss? Their experience of the grace they have known in the midst of their confinement . . . the reality of suffering and how they deal with their own troubles in the light of their faith . . . what brings them joy. The production team might invite people unable to attend Sunday worship to share on video their favorite scripture passage and what it means to them. The team members might inquire about the confined parishioner's experiences of holy baptism and holy communion or record their memories of Christmas, Easter, or the church they may have attended when they were children.

In addition to recording these kinds of testimonies and stories, the church production team might ask those with whom they visit to offer on-camera their own petitions for what or for whom they wished the church to pray. These video-recorded petitions could then be woven into the live prayers of the people on the following Sunday. The production teams might even invite parishioners confined at home to be videotaped reading aloud an upcoming lectionary text for inclusion in that Sunday's worship, an idea Pastor Kent Wilson passed along to me. Or, the production team might simply invite each person they visit to record a single greeting or ritual formula, such as "Peace be with you," or a single word, such as "Amen" or "Alleluia." A video montage of people speaking these phrases or words could serve as liturgical media art at an appropriate time in a service.

In short, these video elements featuring members otherwise physically absent from Sunday worship might be incorporated as part of the congregation's gathering rites, as a proclamation of scripture, as an element of a sermon, as one of the prayers of intercession, as a post-communion meditation, as part of the announcements, or as a sending word at the conclusion of the liturgy.

Making connections between those present and those absent from eucharist is an ancient Christian practice, recorded as early as Justin Martyr's writings in the second century. Worshipers carried the bread broken from worship to those unable to be with the praying community. Following this ancient custom, at the end of the distribution of communion in worship, some members could go directly to visit those unable to attend and to bring them communion. They might also bring items particular to the liturgical year, such as palm branches from Passion Sunday or baptismal water used during the Easter season for members' remembrance of their baptism. The church newsletter, a video bulletin of parish activities, or video greetings from church members could also be delivered to homebound members.

Now possible

A less media-intense way of including those absent from worship for whatever reason, of course, is to incorporate photographs of them during prayers of intercession, during announcements of those sick or hospitalized, or during a liturgy of healing. In a large Australian Roman Catholic parish, photographs of the sick and those who have recently died are regularly included in the pre-liturgy announcements. People tend to recognize faces more quickly than names, especially in a large community. Pastoral leaders have discovered that showing such photos (with permission of those photographed or of their loved ones) helps connect those absent with the rest of the praying community.

When the saints go marching in

Another occasion for the inclusion of photographs of people is All Saints Sunday. Congregations celebrate this day in different ways. Some read aloud names of the deceased as music plays quietly in the background. Becoming more common in some congregations is the practice of bringing photos of loved ones to church and placing them in various locations around the worship space. Alternately, submitted photos could be scanned and edited into an artfully designed media sequence that could be used as a media meditation during an instrumental or choral offering of "For all the saints," "Jerusalem, my happy home," or another appropriate hymn. I once created a customized litany remembering the saints for my children's choir to sing that included a congregational refrain: "Oh, when the saints go marching in." A church could create its own litany giving thanks for its departed saints. With a well-known refrain, the assembly could easily sing its part while watching photographs of all those whom members wished remembered. A media communion of saints could include images of saints ancient and modern. It could also incorporate photographs of people in the news who had died that year, both those well-known and those unknown other than from news photos or footage of the disaster that took their lives. For inspiration on how to honor those who have gone before us, watch the beautiful tributes shown at the end of every year on *CBS Sunday Morning*.

Quality assurance

Saints, it has been said, are ordinary people who do things extraordinarily well. As envisioned in this essay, media ministers are ordinary people who are willing to make an extraordinary commitment to integrating media art into worship in ways that are liturgically appropriate. Along with that commitment comes another: to be discerning in the selection and production of media art so that only what meets accepted communal standards for media production and aesthetic quality is used.

In preparing this book, I have consulted with colleagues who have plenty of experience in integrating media into worship and who were willing to share advice on avoiding some common pitfalls. One colleague is Rev. Dr. Troy Messenger, the director of James Chapel at Union Theological Seminary in New York City. We have talked about what media works in worship. We have also addressed what does not work in *any* worship service: inept or ill-considered integration of media. Messenger related one such case. "Just before a noontime service, a student comes to us with scores of images he wants played continually on a loop throughout the service. This media is not helpful to worship." Why? Could not these images serve as environmental art? Not if they do not belong there. "The images are not referred to during the service and have no connection with the liturgical action," Messenger added. Another common mistake he reports is poor video production quality: video that has audio too low or too noisy to be heard clearly or video backgrounds behind people that are so bright their faces consequently cannot be seen. After many years of working with media in seminary worship services, Messenger advises that media needs to be not only liturgically appropriate and well integrated, but it also needs to be competently produced.

Liturgical media art can help lead a community from one segment of worship to another, connect the community with other communities past and present, serve as a counterpoint that adds a new dimension to a song or prayer, stimulate worshipers to action or interaction, or enrich the liturgy through skillfully produced media art that is apropos and beautiful. Union Theological Seminary students in their introduction to worship and preaching course all must tackle creating media for worship. For older adult graduate students this task can be an intimidating one, because they may not have the production skills, even if they have the ability to imagine an approach. For younger students skilled in image manipulation, graphic and video production and editing, this assignment is welcomed. Whether young or old, students in all seminaries and in pastoral ministry programs need exposure to the basic principles and skills involved in liturgically appropriate integration of media art and to the basic principles of liturgical aesthetics.

The quality of liturgical media art requires not only skilled, liturgically savvy producers but also a process for local pastoral and communal discernment. As with a new building or renovated worship space project, "active dialogue within the congregation enriches the design process and helps to ensure its success." Explains *Principles for Worship*, "such conversation leads the community to understand and appreciate the design directions that are undertaken" (application S-22C). In making decisions about media art in worship, basic principles apply, just as they do in the introduction of any liturgical art or in the revision of any church architecture: "The work of designers and artisans begins with the worshiping community and is informed in dialogue with the worshiping community" (application S-23C). Dialogue about media in worship that engages the community can foster occasions for theological reflection that can bear much spiritual fruit.

Theological convictions

The skills, experience, and wisdom of professional graphic designers, photographers, media producers, and art teachers of every medium are invaluable to any community attempting to offer media art in worship. So are those of theologians, scripture scholars, and others trained in various forms of theological reflection. Just as "it is theological conviction . . . that is the driving force in shaping a house for the church" (application S-21B), theological convictions need to drive the creative forces that lead to the integration of media art in worship. Many theological convictions are implicit in the vision I have shared of media art having the potential to be a revelatory liturgical art. Let me make some of them more explicit.

My suggestion that media art can be a "moving word" comes from a theology of revelation. My conviction is that God reveals Godself to us not only in expected locations and extraordinary moments—holy places where God's holy people have gathered—but also in the unexpected locations and ordinary moments of our daily lives. Constantly trying to get our attention, the Holy Spirit sometimes manages to break through the noise of our lives even while we are watching TV at home, enjoying a movie, listening to a song on our iPods®, surfing the Internet, or shooting home video. The Spirit can indeed use even popular media to get through to us, to move us, to help us turn toward the light of Christ. Not just media art, but also the process of selecting and creating it, can help worshipers see and hear God's self-revelation in their lives.

Communal Co-creation is a spiritual communal practice through which God calls us to "Keep awake!" By engaging in this process, participants may become more attentive and ever more watchful for the signs of God in their midst. Over time, participants can become increasingly attuned to the Spirit in their lives and may more regularly intentionally "tune in" to God's wavelength to hear God's word.

Of course, Communal Co-creation is founded upon an ecclesiology (theology of the church) that is radically inclusive, collaborative, and nonhierarchical. This ecclesiology places great emphasis on the assembly as the *ekklesia* whose principal purpose is to worship and praise God. I see people who contribute to the selection, creation, and evaluation of liturgical media art as being disciples-on-mission, members of a community, a *koinonia,* who have responded to a call to serve, *diakonia.* Whether their mission involves hitting the record button on their mini-videocam, listening to an elder tell her story during an interview, or editing children's art for a baptismal media meditation, they do serve.

Who we are as church and how we behave in relationship with

one another are integrally related. The ecclesiology that grounds Communal Co-creation also implies a deeply held theological ethic. As the body of Christ today, we are responsible to work together, to use our gifts and resources however we can, for the good of the whole church, the whole world, and all of creation. Through our arts, we can make a difference. We can work for and with those people whose gifts, resources, and dignity have been demeaned, diminished, or stolen from them. We cannot make just pretty video; we must make truthful video for their sake, as well as ours. We cannot just make useful media art; we must strive to make art that provides beauty, too, including the terrible kind of beauty that can convict us.

Foundational to my convictions about media art in worship is a theology of art. A few years before his death, Jesuit theologian Karl Rahner wrote, "theology cannot be complete until it appropriates [the] arts as an integral moment of itself and its own life, until the arts become an intrinsic moment of theology itself" ("Theology and the Arts," *Thought*, March 1982, p. 24). Rahner most likely would not have understood media as a potential art at all, but I do think his words about the arts can apply to the diverse forms of media art. Great art, he wrote in an essay on "Theology and the Arts," can be:

> so inspired and borne by divine revelation, by grace and by God's self-communication, that they communicate something about what the human really is in the eyes of God which cannot be completely translated into verbal theology. If theology is not identified *a priori* with verbal theology, but is understood as [our] total self-expression insofar as this is borne by God's self-communication, then religious phenomena in the arts are themselves a moment within theology taken in its totality ("Theology and the Arts," p. 25).

In the three decades during which I have been creating and reflecting upon media art of all kinds for a variety of purposes, I have many times known that "moment within theology," that moment when media becomes *art* filled with God's self-communication, that moment of transcendence when I have learned something "about what the human really is in the eyes of God."

Some years ago I discovered the work of Lutheran theologian and professor Joseph Sittler and recognized in his writings an expansive, integrated theology of grace and theology of creation that can speak to film, video, and digital media arts of all kinds. "The common life is the 'happening place'" of grace, he wrote (*Evocations of Grace: The Writings of Joseph Sittler on Ecology, Theology, and Ethics,* 2000, p. 156). His vision allowed no polarization between God-created nature and human-created culture, which would include today's media technology and media arts. He understood "nature" as encompassing "not only the biological and physical world, but also the 'artificial' world of art, architecture, technology, and social structures. Culture as well as 'nature' is an integral part of creation, and therefore the products of human creativity are also capable of manifesting God's grace" (*Evocations of Grace,* p. 10).

The theological convictions that underpin all of what I have shared draw upon an appreciation for how God can communicate via media. God the Creator is in the midst of all of our communicating what is good, true, and beautiful. Through our media arts, we participate in God's on-going work of creation. Media art that we see on a video monitor or media screen can move us to action, bring us new insight, break through our prejudices, call us to love one another. It can do this, but we must be receptive. When we open ourselves to God, the Holy Spirit breathes new life into us. In such Spirit-filled encounters with media, we can be inspired to be the hands and feet of Christ in the world. Then, we have literally experienced "a moving word."

As individual media producers and as participants in an inclusive Communal Co-creation process that invites worshipers and even outsiders into crafting a moving word for worship, we all are drawn into a profoundly spiritual practice that can be an occasion of grace and can bear much spiritual fruit. We are just at the beginning of learning the art and craft of liturgical media art. Our children and grandchildren will be the ones to move this liturgical art in directions we could never imagine. That prospect is exciting and hopeful. It is an awesome responsibility. In the meantime, parish by parish, we are called to discern the grace-filled movement of the Spirit and how, whether, what, and when media may serve in our liturgies.

A closing challenge

One type of liturgical media art that I hope will emerge in the coming years is the parable. What would serve as parabolic media art for worship? Think of Jesus' parables. They leave us with questions that continue to haunt us long after the story has ended. They take unexpected turns. They feature unlikely protagonists. They turn upside down the usual way of seeing a situation. They predict the high-and-mighty will be laid low and the lowly raised up. Surprise!

Parables capture not only our attention but stretch our imagination to see the reign of God from a different perspective. Today, this parabolic quality is too often lacking in both commercially available and locally produced media for worship. I wish that were not the case, but as a media producer and liturgist I must be honest about how I see the current situation of media produced for worship. Consequently, I leave you with this challenge. How might you contribute to the evolution of liturgical media art that can be tomorrow's liturgical media parable? This new liturgical ministry is potentially open to any and all the saints who live in our media culture, including you. So, consider contributing your gifts and imagination to this good work. In the years to come, we will make mistakes, for sure. We will at times be inept. We will inevitably make poor choices. Yet, in the process of our striving, we, the communion of saints, will create a new form of liturgical art. "Thus says the LORD . . . I am about to do a new thing; now it springs forth, do you not perceive it?" (Isa. 43: 16a, 19a). I do. What about you?

Related Resources

Selected books and articles

Bausch, Michael G. *Silver Screen Sacred Story: Using Multimedia in Worship.* Herndon, VA: Alban Institute Publications, 2002.

Crowley, Eileen D. "Endless crossings: Karl Rahner's theology, communication, and the arts." *Catholic International* 14, no. 4 (August 2003): 96–104.

_____. *Liturgical Art in a Media Culture.* Collegeville, MN: Liturgical Press, forthcoming 2007.

_____. "Media Art in Worship: The Potential for a New Liturgical Art, Its Pastoral and Theological Challenges." Plenary address. Institute for Liturgical Studies, Valparaiso University, Valparaiso, IN, April 20–21, 2004 (www.valpo.edu/ils/publications.php).

_____. "New Media and Normal Mysticism: An Unexpected Gift for Ongoing Spiritual Formation," *New Theology Review* 18, no. 3 (August 2005): 26–31.

_____."The Potential of Media Art in Liturgy," in *Sundays and Seasons Year B 2006* (Minneapolis: Augsburg Fortress, 2006): 14–16.

_____. "Visual Art for Advent: 'Prepare the Way. . . .'" *New Theology Review* 18, no. 4 (November 2005): 86–89.

Crowley-Horak, Eileen. "New Media in Worship," *Eucharistic Ministries* 226 (January 2003): 4–5.

_____. *Testing the Fruits: Aesthetics as Applied to Liturgical Media Art.* Unpublished dissertation. Union Theological Seminary, New York City, 2002. Available via subscription Web site, www.lib.umi.com/dissertations, ProQuest ID no. 726435071, publication no. AAT 3048887, ISBN 0493632174.

_____. "The TV Culture and Its Effects on Worship," *Proceedings of the North American Academy of Liturgy* (1996): 63–76.

Eason, Tim. *Media Ministry Made Easy: A Practical Guide to Visual Communication.* Nashville: Abingdon Press, 2003.

Hutchinson, Cathy. "Experiential Video: Churches Are Moving from Static Information Transfer to Creating Visual Experiences." *Technologies for Worship Magazine* (March 2005): 48–50, 52, 54.

Iles, Chrissie. *Into the Light: The Projected Image in American Art 1964–1977.* New York: Whitney Museum of American Art, 2001. Exhibit and accompanying exhibit book.

Koster, Steven. "Leading with Light: Practical Ideas for Using Video Projection in Worship." *Reformed Worship* 76 (June 2005): 39–41.

Riddell, Mike, Mark Pierson, and Cathy Kirkpatrick. *The Prodigal Project: Journey into the Emerging Church.* London: SPCK, 2000.

Rush, Michael. *New Media in Art,* 2nd ed. London: Thames and Hudson, 2005.

Sample, Tex. *Powerful Persuasion: Multimedia Witness in Christian Worship.* Nashville: Abingdon Press, 2005.

_____. *The Spectacle of Worship in a Wired World: Electronic Culture and the Gathered People of God.* Nashville: Abingdon Press, 1998.

Schultze, Quentin J. *High-Tech Worship? Using Presentational Technologies Wisely.* Grand Rapids, MI: Baker Books, 2004.

Wilson, Len. *The Wired Church: Making Media Ministry.* Nashville: Abingdon Press, 1999.

Wilson, Len, and Jason Moore. *Digital Storytellers: The Art of Communicating the Gospel in Worship.* Nashville: Abingdon Press, 2002.

Selected media ministry resource Internet sites
www.alternativeworship.org
www.churchmedia.net
www.theworkofthepeople.com
www.worshipmedia.com

Church media magazines
Church Production Magazine (www.churchproduction.com)
Technologies for Worship Magazine (www.tfwm.com)
Vision Magazine (www.fowler.com)

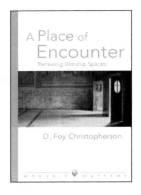

A Place of Encounter: Renewing Worship Spaces
by D. Foy Christopherson

House, temple, theatre, warehouse, courtroom, auditorium, TV studio, or lecture hall? River or baptistery or pool? Dining room or catacomb? House of God or house of the church? In its 2000-year history the church has tried on many buildings, and is ever seeking a more comfortable skin. Exactly what that skin will look like is guided by how the church understands itself, by how it worships, and by what it understands its mission to be. *A Place of Encounter* brings clarity and insight to congregations and individuals who are interested in exploring how our worship spaces serve, form, and proclaim.

0-8066-5107-5

Why Worship Matters

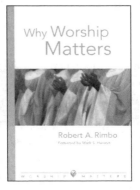

by Robert A. Rimbo
Foreword by Mark S. Hanson

Why Worship Matters is the first volume in a series centering on the Renewing Worship project of the Evangelical Lutheran Church in America. This little volume is a conversation-starter for those who want to look at the assembly's worship in very broad terms. It also invites reflection on the needs of the world, individuals, the church, and society in light of the assembly's central activity, worshiping God.

08066-5108-3

A Three-Year Banquet: The Lectionary for the Assembly

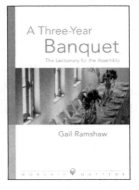

by Gail Ramshaw

A Three-Year Banquet invites the entire worshiping assembly, lay and clergy, to understand and delight in the three-year lectionary. The study guide explains how the Revised Common Lectionary was developed and how the gospels, the first readings, and the epistles are assigned. Further chapters describe many ways that the three readings affect the assembly's worship and the assembly itself. Like food at a banquet, the fare we enjoy in the lectionary nourishes us year after year.

0-8066-5105-9

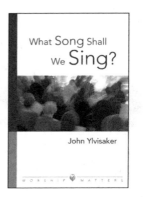

What Song Shall We Sing?

by John Ylvisaker

Much has been written about worship wars and the perceived need for recognizing and implementing different styles of music in the service, whether it be quiet, unaccompanied singing at the one extreme or bands powered by electric guitars and synths at the other. Less has been written about fusing musical styles. This book explores the way hymns are put together and how the fusion technique can heal the wounds of the worship wars. A look at the changing role of vocal and instrumental leadership becomes part of the discussion, with the goal being to bring people together through music.

0-8066-5149-0

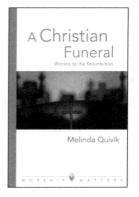

A Christian Funeral: Witness to the Resurrection

by Melinda Quivik

It is one thing to simply bury the dead. It is another to participate in a liturgy that celebrates with honesty the life that has ended, engages the pain of the loss, and proclaims the Christian hope in the resurrection. Because we don't talk very well about the questions raised by death—either in our culture or in our churches—this book invites you to learn some of the history and theology surrounding concepts of the afterlife so that you will be better equipped to plan a funeral that is not simply a utilitarian exercise but a vital and essential font of faith.

0-8066-5148-2

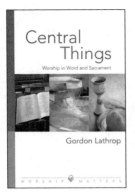

Central Things:
Worship in Word and Sacrament
by Gordon Lathrop

The central things of Christian worship are these: an open and participating community gathered in song and prayer around the scriptures read and preached, around the baptismal washing, enacted or remembered, around the holy supper, and around the sending to a needy world. These things may be done in diverse ways, in diverse cultural situations, responding to diverse times. But they nonetheless unite Christians throughout the world. Taken seriously, they may shape the spirit and the details of our worship. They are a gift of God for the life of the world. By them God continually brings people into faith and so into hope and love.

0-8066-5163-6

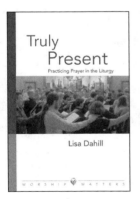

Truly Present:
Practicing Prayer in the Liturgy
by Lisa Dahill

Humans hunger for contemplative prayer. In this readable and practical volume Dahill discusses the need for rediscovering such prayer forms in the ELCA, and introduces Lutheran liturgical spirituality very broadly. Each chapter is devoted to one prayer practice grounded in the liturgy and shows how each contemplative practice both roots within and in turn also deepens our experience of worship.

0-8066-5147-4

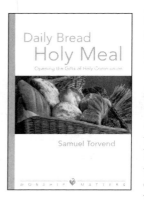

Daily Bread, Holy Meal: Opening the Gifts of Holy Communion

by Samuel Torvend

Daily Bread, Holy Meal invites Christians to reconsider the significance of eating and drinking with Jesus of Nazareth in a world of great need. Drawing on recent biblical and historical studies, this exploration of the Eucharist asks the seeker in every Christian to consider the ecological, theological, communal, and ethical dimensions of the Lord's supper. Through a careful weaving of biblical passages, medieval poetry, Luther's writings, familiar hymns, and newly-written liturgical texts, each chapter unfolds another "gift" of the Holy Communion and the sometimes troubling questions each one raises for individuals who live in a fast food culture yet seek community around a gracious table.

0-8066-5106-7

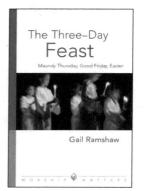

The Three-Day Feast: Maundy Thursday, Good Friday, Easter

by Gail Ramshaw

An introduction to the great Three Days in the church's year that celebrate Christ's passage from death to life. Using the motifs of "telling the story" and "enacting the meaning," Ramshaw illuminates the significance of each day's worship and makes plain the history, symbolism, meaning, and centrality of these core days of the church's life together.

0-8066-5115-6